Praise for *The Corner Shop*

'Part memoir, part social history, *The Corner Shop* is a
gentle, charming and at times poignant look at our nation
of shopkeepers . . . human, accessible and informative, it's
a nuanced exploration of part of British Asian life that
has long been stereotyped – and therein lies this book's
strength'
Nikesh Shukla, *Observer*

'A delightful story of growing up "above the shop"'
Nigel Slater

'One of the best books I've read of the immigrant
experience in this country . . . it's the detail that makes
it . . . a subtle, enjoyable book'
Daily Mail

'A story of assimilation and triumph'
Radio Times

'Sharma cleverly links her own memories of shop-bound
life with the last 50 years of British history'
Spectator

'Full of life, characters, gossip and all the richness of the
local community'
Sir David Jason

'A compelling, full selection box of a story'
Sanjeev Kohli

'I loved it cover to cover'
Angela Clutton, author of *The Vinegar Cupboard*

The Corner Shop

Shopkeepers, the Sharmas and the making of modern Britain

Babita Sharma

TWO
ROADS

First published in Great Britain in 2019 by Two Roads
An Imprint of John Murray Press
An Hachette UK company

This paperback edition published in 2020

1

A CIP catalogue record for this title is available from the British Library

Paperback ISBN 978 1 473 67323 6
eBook ISBN 978 1 473 67324 3
Audio Digital Download ISBN 978 1 473 67325 0

Typeset in Sabon LT by Hewer Text UK Ltd, Edinburgh
Printed and bound by Clays Ltd, Elcograf S.p.A.

John Murray policy is to use papers that are natural, renewable
and recyclable products and made from wood grown in sustainable
forests. The logging and manufacturing processes are expected to
conform to the environmental regulations of the country of origin.

Two Roads
Carmelite House
50 Victoria Embankment
London EC4Y 0DZ

www.tworoadsbooks.com

For Mum & Dad,

my heroes x

Contents

Introduction

I've seen you on a Sunday morning, nipping out to get a pint of milk or to grab a newspaper, thinking no one would notice the oversized coat you grabbed in a hurry, your mismatched pyjamas or your dog-eaten trainers. Your regular appearances throughout my childhood provided me with years of entertainment. I came to know a lot about you; whether your politics leant to the right or left, whether you were gay or straight, and whether you were plagued by cash-flow problems or had enough disposable income to indulge your penchant for Cadbury's Creme Eggs.

I don't work for the secret services, nor do I have special access to you and your family's data. I come from a hidden world: I am the daughter of shopkeepers. For more than a decade we, a family of five, ate, slept, lived and worked in a corner shop. We served you and you gave us business but there was a world beyond the counter that you never knew.

My childhood story is about more than just transactions involving pints of milk and packets of cigarettes; it's integral to the story of Britain itself. It encompasses war and colonialism, the nation's love–hate relationship with immigration, its fluctuating economic fortunes, and it shines a bright light on what people really thought about the politics of the day.

Choose any city upon our clouded hills and you will find us there. We are dotted all over Britain, but the humble corner shop attracts little attention. They have existed on our streets for more than a hundred years, and walking in and out of one may be as normal to you as brushing your teeth, but this tiny space represents all of Britain's highs and lows, past, present and future. The shabby shelving, the chaotic displays of greetings cards and the tins of dog food tumbling to the ground actually represent the cornerstones of community life. The corner shop is a place where daily politics are still deliberated, where the brief exchange of money sparks a priceless debate about the front-page headlines. Regardless of our race, age or gender, the corner shop remains the one place where we all rub shoulders with each other, as well as with the dutiful shopkeeper.

Pete was a regular in our shop. A builder from Reading, he would prop up the counter, chatting to Mum, hoping to catch a glance of hazel-eyed Emily the supply teacher as she came by to collect her copy of *Woman's Own*. Emily would often leave the shop a shade of rose blush under her long, flowing blonde locks and smile embarrassedly at Mum, who would act as if she had seen or heard nothing of the shameless flirting that had taken place. Pete never did get far with Emily, but from a six-year-old's perspective it was marvellous entertainment. Almost as entertaining as minding the shop floor when sixteen-year-old Mark would tiptoe to reach the top-shelf magazines, insisting he was eighteen, only to be turned away when he brought his copy of *Playboy* to the counter. If only his mum hadn't paraded him to all and sundry outside the corner shop when he was born sixteen years and three months earlier, then my parents might not have known and might have dutifully fulfilled his teenage need for a porn mag.

Understanding customers' daily habits became a fact of my childhood. It opened up a secret door to all the goings-on around me. When I began writing this book I knew that, as a former corner shop kid, I was still bound by a particular code of conduct. Because not only is every shopkeeper and his family entrusted with the supply of your groceries and the delivery of your non-crumpled Sunday paper, we are also the custodians of your personal secrets. We must never reveal the clandestine habits of our customers – unless, of course, we change the names of the people concerned to write a book. So Mark, as I am now calling you, your teenage addiction to porn mags will not be revealed now that you're a sitting member of Parliament. Don't worry: your secret is safe with us.

From the forties to the noughties and beyond, the trusted corner shop was there for all our daily needs, and for many families like mine, it was also their introduction to modern Britain. Perhaps your shopkeeper resembles my mum and dad; born in India, they faithfully served as shopkeepers in Reading for more than twenty years. Or maybe the person behind your local shop counter is from Poland or Afghanistan, with his or her own story of immigration and survival.

Whoever the person behind the counter is, they have taken on a role that remains essentially unchanged. I grew up in 1980s Britain, and corner shop life was a window onto a time when the country was dealing with racial tension, recession and the policies of Margaret Thatcher. Maggie, as I'll refer to her in this book, was herself the daughter of a shopkeeper, and she too would have learnt much about the people she served in her father's shop in Grantham in the 1940s. While in power, Maggie presided over a monumental shift in the way we shop – and also dealt the biggest blow to corner shop existence with a repeal of the Sunday trading laws. As this book reveals, the key to survival for a shopkeeper is appreciating how a wolf can arrive dressed in sheep's clothing.

The big supermarkets disguising themselves under the banners of 'little', 'local' and 'express' have as yet been unable to replicate the unique bond between shopkeeper and customer, where a smile will always greet you whether it's 6.30 in the morning or 11 o'clock at night, and where they know your name and your favourite tipple. It's all part of being in the corner shop club. The death of the corner shop has been predicted by many along the way,

but in the face of stiff competition the years of unconditionally serving a nation at all hours of the day are paying
off. There are currently 30,000 local independent shops
across Britain and the corner shop market is expected to
increase by 17 per cent to £44 billion over the next five
years. Not bad for an industry based on making small talk
with you as you peruse the aisles in search of that emergency bag of sugar.

I spent most of my formative years embarrassed by the
mundane activities of shop life, and I'd often daydream of
a time when we as a family might break free from the
rigmarole of early morning wake-up calls. I would try and
convince my schoolmates that my parents were in 'business', but my little lie would be blown apart when they
walked into the shop to be greeted by my so-called high-
flying business parents demanding 10p for a sickly coloured
ice-pop that would turn the tongues of Caversham's children bright blue.

Then something changed, and as I got older I fell in
love with it. My hang-ups about being a corner shop kid
have been enthusiastically replaced by a sense of awe for
the little place that was home. I realised that my upbring-
ing was part of an extraordinary story that very few
people really knew much about. Walking in and out of a
corner shop doesn't tell you what life is really like inside
one of the country's most familiar places. To be part of its
history fills me with an immense pride, knowing that for
decades it has served a nation unconditionally and continues to do so on a daily basis.

My memories of life in a corner shop are so vivid that I doubt they will ever leave me. I haven't forgotten your late-night sojourn to the shop in dirty boots just as we'd cashed up, which meant our bedtime was delayed while Mum and Dad mopped muddy footprints off the floor for a third time that day. But those footprints were just one small mark in a much greater picture: people all over Britain have such affection for this bastion of British life. We all have a corner shop story to tell.

A work colleague fondly recounted tales of his Italian immigrant family, two generations of corner shop owners in London. Pete nostalgically remembers the bestseller in his father's shop: the Snowball. At tuppence a cup, thousands of shoppers would devour Vic Difolco's lemonade topped with scoops of ice cream that became a notorious must-have on the streets of Bermondsey in the late 1960s.

Kate, my publisher, shared the story of how when her flatmate was locked in their bathroom it was the local shop that was the go-to place for some kind of door-opening device to rescue her. In a surprise addition, the shopkeeper offered his services and managed to successfully rescue the flatmate from the confines of the bathroom. And my sister's mother-in-law, Brenda, remembers her mum counting out the ration coupons at the counter of their local shop in 1953 and safeguarding a month's supply of cheese before four-year-old Brenda devoured the entire lot in one sitting.

The corner shop is a unique kind of place – somewhere

you can grab a random Christmas decoration in July, or always find vanilla essence (it's past its sell-by date, but at least they have some!). It's also somewhere that can leave you with a lot of questions: Why is it that trying to find something as ordinary as half a dozen eggs becomes a quest that rivals an episode of *The Crystal Maze*? Who runs a place like this anyway? How can they survive? What is that smell? And how do they stay awake?

The humble corner shop is at times the most foreign of places, yet also the most British of institutions. Look beyond the advert-filled shop windows and broken door-frames and you'll discover a human story that is every bit as remarkable as the history it rests upon. It's time to salute the unsung corner shop, working doggedly every day to make a profit from your countless pyjama-clad visits.

1

Asian Invasion

'Invasion', noun: An unwelcome intrusion into another's domain

No one in the history of mankind has ever said, 'When I grow up I want to own a corner shop, work for fourteen hours a day, seven days a week and never take a holiday.' Or that holidays are overrated, right? And that the best use of one's spare time is to spend it helping out in a corner shop, offering services for free and learning the skills needed to keep a nation happy. And yet that's exactly what my parents, and so many like them, spent their working lives doing. It wasn't, however, a lifelong ambition fulfilled or a dream that became a reality – being a shopkeeper was purely down to a set of circumstances that had presented itself as a tidy package at the right time.

In the summer of 1964 the Delhi sunshine was predictably unbearable, tapping Dad on the shoulder, trying to warn him about the choices he was about to make. But

they went unnoticed as the twenty-four-year-old continued to plot the course of an overseas adventure to a place
of mediocre food and bad weather.

Dad didn't take much notice of what might lie ahead in
a foreign place called England. He hurriedly filled out a
form that was to change his and his future family's life
forever. A two-page document sealed with the crest of the
British High Commission in India took Dad around an
hour to complete before he rushed to meet his friends at
the local wrestling club, where they would contort their
bodies into vulgar shapes and then slam into each other
for fun.

There are certain skills you need to be a corner shop
owner, but none of them were listed on the employment
form that Dad filled out; rather, it resembled a dinner
invitation:

> *The British government humbly requests the pleas-
> ure of your company to help secure the future of the
> British economy, and we will not take no for an
> answer.*

Of course, it wasn't written quite like this, but the urgency
for attendance was palpable with every printed word.
Britain was in need of help to bolster its workforce in the
factories that were expanding across the land, and the
Commonwealth was deemed a good place to begin a
huge recruitment process. Dad was far from alone, scrib-
bling away on a few sheets of cheap white paper:

thousands of men and women across the Commonwealth were all wrangling with the same bureaucratic
exercise.

The most detailed part of the application form was
reserved for a section labelled 'Proof of UK Residency'.
Get this bit right and it would allow you to skip towards
the promise of a new adventure. In this respect, Dad had
every reason to be excited and just a little bit smug. He
knew his application was a done deal thanks to his sister
and brother-in-law, who were already living and working
in the UK.

The years spent jostling with his mates in the wrestling
club were about to be put to good use. He secured an
employment voucher in 1965 by convincing a bunch of
faceless officials that he was the right man to do some
honest manual labour, and his passage was smoothed by
his relatives in the UK vouching for his credibility in the
way only family can. Under different circumstances, their
glowing reference might have aroused suspicion. But
Commonwealth workers were in demand, and no alarm
bells rang.

It's also possible that a UK immigration official took
pity on him when the proof of residency revealed he'd be
staying with his sister in the 'glamorous' location of
Slough. My aunt was an animated writer with a vivid
imagination and in her letters to Dad she loved to tell a
positive tale about the new turf she called home. It would
be years before he discovered for himself just how glamorous a location Slough really was . . .

Dad had a carefree notion that he was going to check out what Britain had to offer for a few years and then return home with a bucketload of experience and pick up life as before. In January 1965 he boarded a dodgy Middle East airliner that was packed like a tin of sardines, wearing a smile that hid a bag of nerves. A new generation of soon-to-be shopkeepers were boarding planes, one after another, carrying return tickets that they would never use.

It was a bleak winter's day when Dad first set foot in a country that was, he thought, quite unremarkable on the face of it. But within weeks of being here, this skinny Asian lad from the Punjab would witness one of the greatest displays of pomp and ceremony a nation could muster. Eighteen days after he arrived the country fell into a period of deep mourning. It was not lamenting the arrival of thousands of immigrants who were about to change the face of Britain forever (that would come later): the country was saying goodbye to a fallen hero.

Winston Churchill suffered a stroke and died on 24 January 1965. The nation's grief was for the death of not only one of its greatest prime ministers, but also – as one commentator remarked at the time – of Britain's imperial past. Here now, though, stood an army of thousands of immigrant workers, including my father, who were about to contribute to British society in a way that would surely make Churchill proud. The government had decided to use its colonial ties to encourage large numbers of workers and their families to come to these shores, squeezing Britain's imperial legacy for every shred of possibility to help in the reconstruction of the economy after a costly war.

How the tables had turned: almost eighteen years after the British had left India and ruthlessly split her in two, here they were, her former rulers and colonial masters, asking India to help repair a serious gap in the UK job market. If only the Indians had been more gung-ho they would've told them to stuff their plea for assistance up their colonial backsides. But new India and its neighbour Pakistan were not in a position to be so cocky. Both countries were still finding their feet and navigating uncharted waters after a vicious and costly separation.

The partition of India had seen Britain orchestrate and preside over the greatest mass migration in modern history, the like of which has never been seen again. The scars were still raw. Dad had crossed over from what is now Pakistan to India at the age of four. The whole family had had no alternative other than to completely uproot their lives. They were living in a new uncertain chaos that unfolded during the brutal partition of India. They were refugees, but they didn't know it.

The plan to split India apart was a hurried and ill-thought-out one, devised by the British to bring about independence and provide a quick exit to the rule of the British Raj. In practice, it drew a line straight through the heart and soul of a nation and split apart our ancestral home of Punjab. Hindus like Dad living in the newly formed Pakistan were pushed across the border in their millions and on the other side, millions of Muslim

13

families were being forced the other way into new territory. Based solely on their religious background a mass exodus of people took place at the India–Pakistan border, with catastrophic consequences. Neither the British nor the rest of the world could have predicted the ensuing bloodbath.

The true extent of the sectarian killings during the time of Partition remains unknown, but conservative estimates put the loss of life at around two million people. And Dad was one of at least fifteen million Indians who were displaced at this time. He was also one of many who witnessed the death and destruction of Partition first hand. To observe the injustices of the world inflicts a wound that nestles itself deep within, never to be spoken of again.

And even twenty years later, any chance to escape those memories and dull the pain was to be grabbed with both hands. After all, escape was an easier option than facing up to catastrophic childhood trauma. Though he never spoke about what he witnessed, Dad would always tell his three daughters that we had no idea how lucky we were when we'd complain about him making us mop the shop floor.

Trauma often results in a wry sense of humour and Dad loves to tell us his favourite story about how he ended up spending the best years of his adult life serving a community from behind a shop counter: 'Let me tell you the one about the hand that strikes a nation and is responsible for the displacement of millions of people. In a sick twist of fate, the same hand reaches out desperately seeking a solution to its own domestic crisis and asks me, a young lad, to help!'

The tale is about as amusing as mopping the shop floor is when you're a teenager.

There is an art to floor-mopping and my parents spent years perfecting it. I'd compliment them further on their skills if only it had made the slightest bit of difference to excusing my sisters and me from doing the chore. It didn't! Mopping the floor at closing time became our domain as soon as we were taller than the mop stick and had acquired the strength needed to squeeze the dirty water from the mop into the galvanised bucket with its welded wringer. It is one of the most mundane chores of shop life, and it always took at least forty minutes to diligently scrub away every trace of the hundreds of dirty feet that had crossed the threshold earlier.

Then there was always one customer who within seconds of us completing the task would beg to be served a desperately needed packet of cigarettes. My parents always obliged when the customer used their charm: 'Oh please, Mrs Sharma, it will only take a minute.' But that minute would feel more like an hour when each footstep slowly turned a gleaming floor to a messy mix of bleach and footprints. God only knows why the late customer would feel it necessary to zig-zag the shop floor instead of using the most obvious straight-line route to the counter. Their departure would see them almost always choose an entirely different path to the exit, browsing the other items on the way as if we had all the time in the world to wait for this inconsiderate chancer. This long-winded goodbye would demand that the process begin again with another mop of the entire shop floor from start to finish.

Floor-mopping skills were not on the hurried invite issued to Dad in 1964, but they remain part of an unwritten set of corner shop duties that is passed down through the generations. Fortunately, I could share the pain of this roster of tasks with my two sisters and, crucially, being born last meant I could dodge some of the most laborious jobs by claiming I just didn't have the strength to manage them.

But I am getting ahead of myself. In the 1960s, when the government sought to bring in foreigners to the labour market, it was to work in the jobs where native Brits were lacking. What the country didn't need at that point were more shopkeepers – there were plenty of white folk already doing a sterling job in the general stores of Great Britain.

There was, however, an urgent need of assistance in the country's factories, textiles mills and hospitals. A sense of enthusiastic despair underpinned the recruitment drive. There was no other choice: the government was stuck. Luckily, the RSVPs started rolling in. People took up the call to arms in significant numbers and the government at the time didn't seem too concerned by the influx of immigrants and more preoccupied with getting the job done.

The increase in the number of immigrant workers wasn't a result of the locals being unwilling to do the jobs that were available; in fact, there was little need for them to apply at all. Between 1950 and 1973, unemployment averaged around 2 per cent and there were fewer than a million people out of work.* The country was enjoying a period of almost full employment, and for its citizens to be in work and out of trouble would usually produce some respite for the government. Economic growth brought an increase in wages and people enjoyed a spectacular rise in income. Prime Minister Harold Macmillan said Britain had 'never had it so good'.

But demand was outstripping productivity and the fear of the silence of an empty production line was sending shivers down the spine of a country that could no longer continue to turn out achievements such as Brunel's railways and Telford's roads; industrialisation had created the technologies, but there were simply not enough workers to man it. Britain was in trouble, and the problems began long before an ethnic minority group could be blamed for stealing all the jobs from British workers.

There was a solution, however: shift work. Working round the clock was seen as an effective way of maximising productivity, but such a prospect created a whole new issue – who on earth would want to work all hours of the day and night?

* 'Whatever happened to full employment?' Lord Skidelsky, BBC News, 13 October 2011

Like a school kid avoiding class, Britain's workforce refused to take on the extra work. Why break your back when you could happily sit on your sofa with the heater on, enjoying a cup of Ovaltine? Any person willing to work through the night for little in return was either stupid . . . or on to something. Perhaps the nation should have known then what was to come. 'The early bird may catch the worm, but the night owl can catch a customer in the wee small hours', as the old corner shop proverb goes. If you were open to the idea of going beyond the parameters of daytime work, you could potentially cross the threshold to a world where pennies become pound notes. British employers soon realised they'd have to bring in labour from overseas to make the concept of the night shift a reality, and the recruitment drive went into fifth gear.

In the 1960s, New Commonwealth citizens were admitted into Britain at the rate of about 75,000 people per year.* Every single person that walked off those planes into the UK was here for a reason, and that reason was money. Both for the government with its labour crisis and for the immigrant embarking on an adventure, this was a clear-cut business transaction: the workers would get jobs, and the authorities would see the Great put back into Britain.

Thanks to the British Nationality Act of 1948 citizens of the British Empire were given the right to live and work in

* 'Bound for Britain', The National Archives

the UK. Formally known as British subjects, all nationals of Commonwealth member states were now part of a family with a shared common citizenship. My mum and dad were not therefore subject to immigration control and could enter and stay in the UK without restriction. The law would soon change, requiring immigrants to have a strong connection to Britain through birth or ancestry, but they got in before the government decided to do away with the employment voucher programme that brought Dad here.

The door to Dad's new life was bright green, just one of many in the rows of Victorian houses in the Berkshire town of Slough. Unremarkable in design, this red-brick terraced house was home to four other family members who had already staked a claim to the best rooms inside. Dad was given the back room; one he thankfully didn't have to share with anyone. At the time, it suited him just fine.

He wrote regular updates to his parents in India, telling them how very much he missed them, and detailing the new world in which he found himself. Not wanting them to worry, he would be sure to sign off on a positive note, reassuring them that all was well.

He lied. He missed walking the mud-clad streets of Delhi, dodging stray dogs and bumping into familiar friendly faces at every corner. Running an errand back home would take at least an hour, as he'd be accosted by passers by asking after the family and enticing him to partake in a quick cup of chai and a chat. He was never alone, and basked in the warmth of being part of an extended family that stretched for miles around him. Having graduated in English from Punjab University, he passed his days working as a labourer in the family's construction business. The work was not for him but he didn't mind the man hours he put in as something inside told him it would be a short-term arrangement. He knew the world was most definitely his oyster and he'd been excited by not knowing what lay ahead. The memories put a bittersweet smile on his face.

For three years after he arrived in the UK, he struggled to suppress the aching loneliness and his memories of a pleasing world of friends and family that he had left behind. As time passed he became more certain than ever that he'd soon be heading home for good, so he decided he would throw himself into the experience of British life, as it was merely temporary. The British government was banking on many immigrants feeling the same, but somehow it didn't work out that way.

Whatever pain Dad was feeling, by the time we came along there was no evidence of it, and he continued a life-long adventure on the shores of Britain, accumulating children, grandchildren, three corner shops, a free bus pass and a firm sense of what it means to be British.

You don't just rock up to a shop and think about walking in and taking over. Well, you could, but that would be naïve. To be a shopkeeper takes guile, guts and resilience, and if ever there was a training camp for running a corner shop successfully, the factory floors of 1960s Britain were it.

The employment voucher scheme placed Dad in a role at a metal industries plant in Sunbury-upon-Thames, where his isolation was compounded by being just one of two Asian lads among a workforce of hundreds of men.

The faceless bureaucrats didn't appreciate the three-bus, two-hour commute to get there, nor the fact that this twenty-four-year-old who had never stepped foot inside a factory had no idea what a sheet-metal worker's job would entail. Fortunately on this first day he was told rather apologetically that he would now be placed on a different production line as a spray painter. Dad could not hide his delight and, thanks to the genius of a dentist in the 1930s who invented the spray gun that revolutionised painting on a large scale, he didn't mind it. The spray-gun application was much faster than the brush method and Dad was thankful for the leg-up.

Day after day the large metal sheets would chug along the production line and stop at a point where Dad would spray each one in either off-white or grey before pressing the button that would pull it from view, destined for an unknown location. Many of the metal sheets that Dad spray-painted still hang high above the heads of passengers in Terminal 3 of London's Heathrow Airport. Look closely and you might spot an 'I WOZ ERE' etched into one of them by a certain young Asian man in 1965, trying to amuse himself while colleagues kept their distance from him because he looked so very different.

If you were an immigrant in Britain at that time, the chances of gaining a promotion over your white counter-parts were slim. Discrimination was widespread, and when the economy began to slow down in the late 1960s it was invariably black and Asian workers who lost their jobs first. For those who did remain in work, Commonwealth migrants often did twice the amount of shift work as their white British colleagues, and generally earned significantly lower wages.

After three years of non-stop painting, with the three-bus commute from Slough to Sunbury both taking its toll and chewing into his £3 weekly salary, Dad decided it was time to try something that would pay proportionally better for the hours he put in. His search took him just a stone's throw away from his front door.

Slough's expansion in its early years seemed to be the source of much frustration for a future poet laureate who took great issue with the town's economic ambitions:

> Come friendly bombs and fall on Slough!
> It isn't fit for humans now.

Asian immigrants clearly didn't agree and the town proved a popular choice because of its close proximity not only to the capital but also to Heathrow Airport: there was no need to travel far when you were unsure of where to lay your hat. The town was also the source of thousands of jobs, since several companies had chosen Slough Trading Estate – the first and still the biggest of Europe's business parks – as their global headquarters. Unlike Betjeman, who was seemingly struck by the 'menace of things to come', Dad took advantage of all that Slough had to offer.

Mars confectioners had – and still have – their head-quarters in Slough, and Dad had heard great things about the company, which apparently offered a good salary, sick pay and security in retirement. He applied for a job and within a few weeks received notification that his application had been a success with a warm welcome note from the general manager:

> *Welcome to Mars. We are delighted to have you with us. We hope you find your work here as rewarding for a job well done as it is financially. You will have the satisfaction of knowing you are part of one of the most progressive companies in the country, as well as one of the biggest in the confectionery industry.*

The sunshine that radiated off the welcome note made Dad feel instinctively that he was finally in the right place. He would spend the next twenty-five years enjoying every moment of being in the Mars family, with promotion and career progression opportunities in abundance.

However, to begin his Mars career sitting among rows of women as a packer in the Opal Fruits section was a less than glorious introduction: it was usually only women who carried out the low-level work packing sweets on the factory line. What would later prove to be one of our shop's bestselling products was passing through Dad's hands, but at that point he was completely oblivious to the fact that soon he'd be presiding over the company's sales figures rather than preoccupied with its rainbow-coloured packaging.

Dad's time with the womenfolk was brief, and just like the other male packers that had gone before him, within two weeks he was on his way up to giving the women orders as a machine operator. Most of the women on the packing line would spend a lifetime in the role, rarely able to climb the factory ladder to the more prominent position of machine-minder or charge-hand. It was, as Dad pointed out, a sorry state of affairs, as many of the women were incredibly dedicated to the job and, given the chance, they would have made excellent leaders.

It remains a point of great amusement for my friends that I grew up above a sweet shop run by one of my parents, while the other one worked in a chocolate factory. I was by all accounts the luckiest girl in the world.

Mum's invite to the UK was less of an urgent call to duty than the one her husband had received. She walked off the BOAC flight to London in 1970 to join her new husband with excitement and trepidation. Mum had fulfilled the Indian tradition of meeting her life partner through an arranged marriage. The tradition requires a vetting process whereby parents and other relatives decide on a life partner that they deem suitable for their child. The suitability is usually based on religion, education, looks and family pedigree, and, having been vetted by her family, Dad was considered to be an ideal suitor for Mum. She fortunately had the opportunity to either dismiss or agree with the union, and she willingly accepted the proposal. In doing so, though, she had also accepted that her life was about to change considerably.

As a clerical worker Mum had been enjoying living and working in a capital city that at the time was embarking on a new phase of industrialisation. The West still seemed far away but it was making its way to India, with hippies seeking enlightenment and budget travellers and wealthy jetsetters all swayed by the exotic romance of India. But as India attracted foreigners to its shores, the natives were leaving in their thousands.

The economic expansion of Delhi would soon pass Mum by as she opted for very different surroundings. The United Kingdom was not completely unknown to Mum, as uncles, aunts and cousins had made the leap across some five years earlier. They would often share their stories of life abroad, which would always include a description of another rainy, cloudy day, but there was nothing quite like experiencing it first-hand, as she was about to discover. If you ask her how she felt at the time, Mum will simply and diplomatically lament the weather: 'I'd never worn tights before and I couldn't get used to them.' If only the chill factor Mum experienced had come solely from the climate.

Mum was upset by the lack of distinction between the uniform terraced houses in Slough, and the fact that she could only tell her front door from the others by its bright green colour. But as soon as she arrived, Mum quickly realised that there was a strict mantra she must adopt in order to move forward without fuss or emotion – Get On With It. This mantra she recited in her head on an almost daily basis. There was, for her, no other choice but to persevere in the predicament in which she found herself, occupying rented accommodation with four unfamiliar faces from a family that she had married into. With two incomes between them, Mum had no doubt that in a short time they would no longer need to call this house home.

Behind the closed door to the single room that the couple occupied they devised a strategy to survive an environment that was increasingly claustrophobic. Diplomacy. It is perhaps the most valuable skill they learnt to prepare them for a future career as shopkeepers.

While Dad had become very familiar with the West Indian bus drivers on his six-bus round trip to Sunbury, Mum was following in the footsteps of most of the other working women of Britain and taking up the role of packer on a factory line. She was one of hundreds who would spent eight hours a day stuffing and packing thousands of boxes of aspirin for the company Aspro, whose headquarters were also in Slough. If life at home wasn't claustrophobic enough, the building was one of Britain's first examples of a windowless factory, relying on artificial light and ventilation. But the women found solace in each other and enjoyed the animated chat on the production line, exchanging stories and gossiping the hours away.

Then, one Monday morning in 1970, Mum found herself the focal point of the factory gossip. Three weeks into the job, the chargehand's beady eyes caught sight of Mum stalling at the annual health check that was a prerequisite for new employees at the pharmaceutical company. Mum sheepishly stepped back from the chest X-ray machine and urged her friend to go before her after she read a sign that said, 'If you are pregnant, or think you are pregnant, please tell reception.'

She was fully aware that, should the heavens have blessed her with a child, the wrath of the manager would fall upon her as quickly as a submarine with a hole in it would sink to the seabed. Nonetheless, it was a conversation she couldn't avoid:

Boss: 'What seems to be the problem, Mrs Sharma?'
Mum: 'I was just wondering, if someone thinks they
    might be pregnant, whether they should walk into
    the X-ray machine?'
Boss: '*Are* you pregnant?'
Mum: 'No. I'm not sure . . . Maybe.'

The boss's face filled with rage as she accused Mum of lying for not disclosing the possibility of a pregnancy during her interview three weeks earlier. As the blood reached her hairline she couldn't help but throw Mum a parting remark:

'Bloody Indians!'

The comment pricked the ears of an entire workforce, a large proportion of which just happened to be from the Indian subcontinent.

The good news is that although Mum was pregnant, against the odds she was able to stay packing the aspirins into cardboard boxes for another seven months. There was no farewell party when she departed the Aspro building, however. As they slammed the gates shut behind her she vowed never to return to a factory floor again. To say she was missed would be an exaggeration, but the allies that Mum had made on the factory floor spoke of the other women who came after her who at least felt brave enough to divulge their happy news and sidestep the X-ray machine without fear of reprisal.

I think there must have been a supplementary form to the one Dad filled in back in 1964 that went amiss somewhere between the desks of the High Commission in Delhi and London's immigration department. It states how successful applicants may potentially find themselves occupying tiny spaces on the corners of Britain's streets, signing a contract that surrenders the good years of their adult lives to the role of serving others. This contract lasts for approximately twenty-five years and the authorities accept no liability for what might happen during that time.

Had Dad caught sight of the missing pages, he may well have thought twice about filling out the application.

Being a corner shop owner was never in his thinking when he daydreamed about what life outside of Delhi might look like. Shopkeepers in India were not exactly thought of as having achieved very much and were seen as working class, often uneducated folk. As a graduate in English, Dad and his family would never have imagined that he'd make a career out of something that was seen as parochial.

The corner shops of Delhi were abundant, serving a community in much the same way as their British counterparts later would. Stocking food, soft drinks and household goods, they were the go-to place for essential items. However, the general store in Dad's town was organised in a chaotic manner. It would take a while to find a product and it was not uncommon to have to lift one object from another to uncover what you were looking for. Inches of dust would gather on the shelves of the lesser-sold items, but the shopkeeper, Mundun, didn't seem to care, preferring to indulge in daytime naps in the searing heat rather than minding shop.

Mundun, a stocky man in his twenties, was known around town not for selling the essential items of food but for selling paan – this was his shop's unique selling point. Paan is a mixture of betel nut, herbs, spices and often tobacco wrapped in a betel leaf. Served folded into a triangle or rolled, it is spat out or swallowed after being chewed. Dating back to ancient times, paan originated in India before becoming popular throughout Asia. Often used often as a palate cleanser, the tobacco variety acts as a caffeine-like stimulant and is highly addictive. Dad recalls that non-paan eaters would lament at how the ruby red saliva stains would tarnish the sidewalks – a sign of users spitting out the remnants of their habit. Nowadays the spitting of paan juice in public can draw fines as various governments try to tidy up their streets.

Mundun's shop measured 5x3 metres, was made entirely from wood and stood on a narrow footpath, enabling him to serve customers from a front window while observing all the passers by. Mundun enjoyed his little spot of power, attracting young and old men from around the suburb of Dev Nagar eager to satisfy their demand for addictive paan.

In years to come, Dad would realise that having a unique selling point was essential to corner shop survival. Mundun's paan rolling skills were greatly respected and attracted a daily crowd. The palm sized betel leaves would be laid out before Mundun used a thin stick to spread katha (areca catechu) and chuna (slaked lime), which when mixed together produce the notorious redbrick colour paste. Gulkhand – rose petal leaves and sugar – would then be topped with nutmeg, liquorice and anise before adding tobacco, which could be finished with a variety of up to fifteen flavours.

Mundun was not a conventional shopkeeper. After hours he would sit outside his shop and invite the local men in for a few glasses of whisky and a meat-fuelled feast of tandoori chicken, lamb and roti. The men would gather, laughing and telling tales into the wee small hours lit only by a single lightbulb that dangled precariously from the handmade roof. Simply known as 'Mundun's', the store secured its place in the hearts of many. Though it was not a role that Dad had ever aspired to, he grew up with a comforting sense of Mundun being around. He was a constant in many people's lives, an integral part of community life in the way that shopkeepers often are, wherever you are in the world.

Years later, my parents would enter into a corner shop contract of their own. They managed to secure an early release after twenty-two years on the grounds of good behaviour, but that's still longer than the average life sentence in prison. They had also, unknowingly, signed us up to a clause that would place my family on the frontline of community life in Britain, and thanks to events that were unfolding in East Africa, we would not be the only ones.

2

Bloodsuckers

*'Bloodsucker', noun: An insect or other animal that
sucks blood, especially a leech or a mosquito*

Savanna elephants are intelligent, sociable animals native to
Sub-Saharan Africa. The Savanna enjoys living in family
groups and pays no attention to political borders, roaming
large landscapes in search of food and water. The Asian
shopkeeper and the Savanna have a lot in common. Aside
from the healthy disregard for countries' borders, the Asian
shopkeeper, like the elephant, never forgets. If you cut across
them on a street corner they'll clock your address to ensure
your newspaper is delivered a little bit crumpled the next
day. The art of remembering is a welcome skill in the corner
shop trade. Anyone wishing to embark on a career as a shopkeeper would do well to take note of how remembering
moments of misfortune and despair can instil a work ethic
and a determination to succeed no matter what the cost.

If your local shopkeeper happens to be from East
Africa and is called Mr Patel, chances are he will

particularly identify with the skill of never forgetting where you have come from. You may think of a corner shop owner as typically being from India but in fact the origins of the person behind the till is often much more complex than that. The term 'Asian shopkeeper' was adopted by Britain at a time when immigration was at its peak and a link between the corner shop and a particular ethnic group became forever embedded into British life. By the 1960s Indian immigrants to Britain were beginning to take on the many struggling general stores, but they weren't going to be the only ones for long. The immigration from India to Britain was not the only route by which would-be Asian shopkeepers were making their way here. Once here, East African Indians also saw the business potential in the corner shop. But the majority of Britons in the 1970s bundled us all together under a title that did little to distinguish the mass numbers arriving into the UK from a continent that is the largest and most populous in the world.

To call us 'Asian' threw us all into a bracket that was unwilling to distinguish between people who differed quite significantly in areas of language, culture, religion and food. Trust me when I tell you we really don't look the same either. Put a Punjabi, a Gujarati and a South Indian in the same room and you'll see what I mean. Add into the mix some East African Asians and this will again reveal differences that are visible, for example, in the way a man ties his turban – a pointed turban usually indicates the wearer to be from Kenya, for instance, whereas a rounded turban is often worn by Sikhs or Hindus from India.

If you're lucky enough to have attended a number of Indian weddings, you'll have noticed the stark contrasts within the community that are often defined by whether or not the wedding has meat and alcohol. Varying levels of debauchery can be witnessed alongside some very funky dance moves, depending on which part of India you are from.

We are not all technically brown either. A sales assistant who stood perfectly preened behind the beauty counter at Debenhams once told me that I was not on the brown spectrum at all, but that my skin was more a sallow yellow. Who'd have thought the Asian gene pool would have been included in L'Oréal shades of nude?

Being born into a Hindu family originally from the Punjab, I grew up with the understanding that Punjabis were brilliant in most ways. But my family had never shied away from celebrating the differences within the Asian community and any personal allegiances were put aside in the common interest of sharing the corner shop empire. A few years after the Indian inroads into British corner shops began, many of our East African brothers and sisters of Indian origin would soon also enter into corner shop territory and do more than take a slice of the pie, but not before going through an ordeal of their own.

Once described by Winston Churchill as the 'Pearl of Africa', in the early 1970s the tiny East African country of Uganda was about to lose its shine. At the time, Ugandan

Asians were in a unique position of controlling 90 per cent of the country's wealth while numbering only 50,000, making up just 1 per cent of the population.* However, life for the so-called business class of Uganda was about to change dramatically.

General Idi Amin took to the stage on 4 August 1972 dressed in full military uniform; sweat beads on his brow forming like a spider weaving its untimely web. It took the then President of Uganda just five minutes to divide a country along racial lines, proclaiming that Asians had 'kept themselves apart, living and operating in a close community and refusing to integrate'. They were, he said, 'bloodsuckers', and, like chewing gum on the sole of a shoe, the label stuck.

Non-native Ugandans apparently enjoying pots of gold were considered selfish and indulgent, and the government who had fraternised with the Asian 'enemy' began turning its back on the people who had contributed 90 per cent in taxes to the country. Uganda's entire Asian population was given ninety days to pack up their lives and their children, or risk being imprisoned in military camps.

Of course, if there was any bloodsucking going on it was Idi Amin himself who was responsible, since his presidency protected a piece of legislation that was responsible for pushing Asians directly into the path of business.

* 'Ugandan Asians dominate economy after exile', Farhana Darwood, BBC News, 15 May 2016

Thanks to colonial governance, Africans weren't allowed to go into trade and Asians were banned from owning any land. This created a division of labour along racial lines and enabled the Asian community to excel in the only role they were legally allowed to fulfil – business. East African Asians were not so much living in a closed community as inhabiting a space that forced them to unite in the face of growing oppression. The stage had been set for training another category of Britain's future shopkeepers and they didn't even know it.

Uganda's ethnic cleansing was a brutal dismissal of an entire people, and the Africanisation policy had already spread to Kenya and Tanzania. As traumatic as these years were, they could result in the most memorable of reunions in the most unlikely of places . . .

When Mum was starting her new life in the UK, her best friend, my Auntyji, was living in Nairobi on borrowed time. A side note: there is an unwritten code of conduct when you grow up in an Asian family, one of the tenets of which includes bestowing the title of Auntyji or Uncleji on very many people who may not be related to you, familiar or even nice. Everyone is, until you are told otherwise, an aunt or an uncle, and 'ji' is added as a sign of veneration. It *always* gains you extra points on the respect-o-meter. To drop the title was unthinkable, and any blatant disregard for this Asian tradition was a red flag indicating that the kid in question's parents had not brought them up properly, and their life path was leading straight to foul-mouthed alcohol binges on a Saturday night, just like the white kids. So Mum's best friend and her husband were very much given the title of Auntyji and Uncleji. Such were the close ties between our families that, growing up, I was never aware of the lack of blood between us.

Auntyji and Uncleji had discovered a love for East Africa in the sixties after my uncle received a job opportunity that took him from Delhi to Tanzania and eventually from Tanzania to Kenya. It was a chance to leave behind the familiar and work for the government as an internal auditor. Uncle was convinced that the continent would come good on its promise of good fortune and a better quality of life. And it did ... for a while.

Nairobi was my aunt and uncle's home from 1959 to 1969, and in the sixties their life in Kenya was positively thriving. The era of peace and love that was to sweep the shores of America and England in the 1960s began, it seems, in East Africa, where, regardless of race, colour or religion, communities lived harmoniously side by side like an advert for the United Colours of Benetton.

Like many other East African Asians, my cousins enjoyed a comfortable standard of living. A cleaner took care of all the household chores so my aunt could concentrate on raising five children whose memories of Kenya still shine as bright as they did sixty years ago.

The school run was as colourful as the various fruits hanging off the trees. The kids would angle their necks as far back as they could to catch a daily glimpse of the hundreds of bats that would huddle together, obscured by the wide palm trees. School satchels were full of ripe mangoes that kids would wrestle off the trees in preparation for the weekend and the opportunity to grab some sacred family time. And the sound of steam trains, seemingly powered by the smell of fragrant flowers and cooking fires, provided a melodious accompaniment to an exotic safari adventure to Mombasa.

There is, I am told, no other place in the world where the sunset smiles such a bright golden yellow against a deep orange sky. A Kenyan thunderstorm would see the chameleons and children running for cover, giggling in anticipation of Mother Nature's awesome display of lightning and sound. On the street, stalls of fresh vegetables and fruit would stand ready, tempting hands to bring them home on market day. And on every corner, sellers would sing out the food of the day – fresh mogo (cassava) or corn on the cob, grilled to perfection and sprinkled with a touch of love and salt . . .

No week was complete without a sojourn to Thika Falls and a picnic by the lakes where you'd have to hop from leg to leg to avoid the giant red ants hovering round your ankles, eager for their next meal.

However, all this beauty and serenity masked an imminent danger. While children whirled round untroubled on the carousel of freedom, parents smelled fear in the African air, and one summer morning in 1968 a jeep full of soldiers arrived at the family home, bringing with them an army load of trepidation. My aunt screamed at the children to find a safe hiding spot, convinced that the troops were there to round up the family. In fact, earlier that morning a group of monkeys had caused havoc in the area and the soldiers were simply making house-to-house calls to ensure no significant damage had been caused by the feral animals. But though on this occasion it was the monkeys that were taken away, no one really knew who would be next.

The Africanisation policy sweeping across East Africa was moving ever closer, and it had begun to tarnish life in the place that had become home. Asian workers were finding it increasingly difficult to obtain work permits, and this discrimination cut off their ability to make a living. In 1968 around 40,000 Kenyan Asians were made stateless and at least a third of those with British passports headed to the UK.*

A Kenyan superstition says that if a chameleon changes colour before your eyes, you will meet your end. My aunt and uncle had caught sight of the government's swift change of clothes and knew that their African adventure was coming to an abrupt close. By 1969 my uncle had lost his job, and his family of seven had made the decision to head to the UK in search of an opportunity to escape discrimination and to make use of being part of the Commonwealth family. Like my parents, they were able to enjoy the benefits of being Citizens of the Empire

---

* 'The Kenyan Asians, British Politics, and the Commonwealth Immigrants Act, 1968', Randall Hansen (*The Historical Journal*, September 1999)

and enter into the United Kingdom without fear or restriction.

Dressed in clothes fit only for a Kenyan summer's day, they arrived in the UK with very little and the children were not prepared for the winter that was biting Britain in November 1969. Their feet touched ground in London three years after the arrival of my dad, whose entry into the UK had been significantly less dramatic.

What greeted the family was an understanding that life was about to become incredibly difficult in this new country, which bore little resemblance to the place they had left behind. As my uncle set about seeking employment, my aunt had no choice but to join him. For the first time in her life she became a working mum of five children and joined the throngs of immigrants who found sanctuary in one of Britain's hundreds of factories.

Our two families were reunited not against the colourful backdrop of bustling Nairobi or the chilled-out lush green fields of the Punjab but on a rainy, grey day in Hounslow – a place that would become my childhood second home. Leaving Kenya had been a shock to the system, and my aunt would talk to Mum in great detail about how she was overwhelmed by all the jobs she had to do in and outside the home. Life in Kenya was a distant memory, but there was no going back.

My Indian-East-African-(now)British Auntyji would proudly refer to me as her daughter when we bumped into her pals on Hounslow high street doing a food shop. It was always a fascinating day out with Auntyji. I'd tag along carrying her reused plastic carrier bags and watch the precision with which she'd carefully size up a marrow and sniff bunches of coriander on sale at bargain prices.

The vegetable examination would usually take an hour and as a kid I'd marvel at what possible advantage one potato might have over the other as my vision became blurred by the hundreds that were lined up on crates stacked so low you'd be doing squats to reach them. A good workout was had by all, and given this obsession with produce it was perhaps no surprise that these displaced African Asians would soon go into the world of corner shop commerce. After the vegetables had been thoroughly inspected, our tummies would rumble excitedly, knowing what was coming next. It was time to head back to Auntyji's house for the mass preparation of her famous Gobi Paratha.

God placed magic in the fingers of my aunt. Having lived in four different countries she had developed the greatest repertoire in the history of Indian cooking, combining her years of experience in East Africa and her childhood in the Punjab. The entire population of West Hounslow would be treated to the daily aroma of her exquisite home-made food. And like the children following the Pied Piper, unexpected visitors would arrive on her doorstep to enjoy a healthy serving of the home-made Dhokla that she always had on the go, served up with the warmest of smiles. These pocket-sized bright yellow semolina cubes would be accompanied by chutney made from fresh mint that she grew in the garden. And if your luck was in, Auntyji might also have been up late the previous night preparing a dozen or so freshly made Gulab Jamun. These sugar-filled dumplings might have sent your BMI soaring, but they made your taste buds shiver with delight. Her food was pure heaven, the like of which I have never tasted since her death. I miss her.

It's a shame Auntyji's love language of food hadn't been more readily accepted by the powers-that-be back in Kenya. If it had been, perhaps they would have fallen in love with a community that contributed so much to East African life and realised that a mass expulsion of a people was not needed.

During the late sixties and early seventies, thousands of East African Asians went from riches to rags overnight and arrived in the UK with just the clothes on their backs and fifty quid in their pockets. Dismissed for their economic prowess back home, they were nonetheless armed with seasoned entrepreneurial skills – suddenly, a new generation of shopkeepers had arrived on Britain's doorstep.

Many Asians who were expelled from East Africa were flown on special chartered flights to Heathrow, Gatwick and Stansted before being bussed directly to resettlement centres that were set up by the government. Caving in to domestic and international pressure the government, under Edward Heath, accepted that they had a responsibility to accommodate the tens of thousands of African Asians who held British passports.

Sir Charles Cunningham was tasked with heading up the Ugandan Resettlement Board responsible for delivering the government's reception and the resettlement programme. One of the resettlement centres was the ex-RAF base Stradishall near Bury St Edmunds in Suffolk. The base was one of the main homestays for Ugandan Asians who were displaced by Idi Amin but during the peak of arrivals in October 1972, there were reports of overcrowding and poor sanitary conditions.

TV reporter Lawrie Quayle headed to the Heathfield resettlement centre in Honiton, Devon, and interviewed several young arrivals from Uganda, asking them in a very public-service-broadcaster way about the weather and the food. The following is a transcript of the interview that was broadcast in 1972:[*]

LQ: How are you enjoying your first day in Britain?
Asian Woman: Yes. I enjoy it.
LQ: You don't mind the terrible weather?
Asian Woman: No.
LQ: Do you feel cold?
Asian Woman: A little bit.

The footage reveals the nameless Asian woman wearing at least four layers of clothing, and a scarf wrapped around her head as if she's about to embark on a North Pole expedition with Sir Ranulph Fiennes.

* Ugandan Asians at Heathfield Camp, The Box Plymouth, 1972

LQ: How do you relish the British fish and chips –
  have you had any yet?
Asian Woman: No.
LQ: How are they looking after you here at Heathfield,
  okay? Are they looking after you all right?
Asian Woman: Yes. All right.
LQ: What do you think of the British food? You've
  obviously had a few meals here by now. All right?
Asian Woman: Yes. [*Pause*] All right.

It tasted like shit, apparently. Watery soup with stale white bread was the order of the day, alternating between vegetable, tomato (apparently the nicest option) and oxtail (not great for the non-beef-eating Hindus).

Of course, one was thankful to be eating at all, when the alternative was a military camp in Uganda where being fed – or not – was entirely dependent on a prison officer's mood. It was, however, uppermost in the minds of the thousands who were housed in temporary accommodation with little appreciation for what a 'meat and two veg' meal might entail. A ladleful of mashed potato would be slapped onto each metal dinner tray as the displaced queued up patiently to be served by hardened faces who had little time for any requests for a bit of chilli or a dash of extra salt.

Aloo Gobi. Why could they not just serve us some Aloo Gobi? The mere possibility of tasting fried cumin seeds, onions and tomatoes, green chillies, turmeric and salt, smouldering over cauliflower and potatoes on a plate served with Basmati rice as light as a feather pillow, was the only way to keep hearts and minds alive in the bleakness of the shelters.

By 1973 some 30,000 Asians had arrived in the UK, the numbers clearly boosted by the East African exodus of Kenyan, Tanzanian and Ugandan Asians.[*] The old and quintessentially English city of Leicester proved a popular choice for migrants, with around 20,000 Asians heading to the East Midlands to set up home.[†]

Concerns about what a sudden influx of immigrants might do to a city trickled into a meeting room at Leicester City Council. So dire was the perceived problem that an urgent solution was sought, and what better solution could there be than to publish a very public warning? The collective intelligence of the council decided to take out one-page advertisements in the Ugandan press warning Asians that Leicester was full, and they should stay away.

However, the attempt to dissuade the masses had the opposite effect. Quite against its original intention, Leicester City Council ended up provoking what is termed as 'psychological reactance' – a situation wherein people are made aware that information is being kept from them, thus triggering an increased desire to access it. The council was responsible for a perfect own goal. A city that

[*] 'Ugandan Asians: Life 40 years on', Rupal Rajani, BBC News Online, 6 August 2012
[†] 'Asian life: A history of Leicester', Jeevan Panesar, BBC Online

many Asian people had never heard of was now firmly planted in their psyches.

The local councils were not alone in fearing what this latest wave of immigration might mean for Britain. The storm from the skies of East Africa had lost its ferocity by the time it had landed softly on the plains of England. But it brought with it thousands of people to the corners of Britain's streets armed with a business acumen that would arouse jealousy in shopkeepers across the land.

3

A Family Affair

'Know not what your parents can do for you but what you can do for them.'
Mr Sharma, sitting at the family table c.1983

The corner shop is a quintessentially British institution. Though its face has changed from a very white pre-war incarnation to the ideal entrepreneurial gym for hard working immigrants, the passing of time has not altered its unique place in our lives. Margaret Thatcher and I stand at either side of this corner shop spectrum. In the game of 'mine is bigger than yours', we were on a par. Our shops were similar in size and both were on the corners of very busy town streets. One breathed life into an immigrant family while the other housed the future prime minister of England.

Maggie's bedroom window looked out over the high street of Grantham while mine took in the delights of Caversham. Our living quarters above the corner shop would have been designed in an eerily similar way. We were corner shop kids, members of a unique club where family and work life mesh together. An extra pair of hands, or three in my family's case, was utilised in the best possible way by doing shifts on the shop floor. If you weren't busying yourself eating the stock, you'd be stacking it on the shelves. Maggie apparently did much the same: helping her father run a grocery shop at 1 North Parade.

Living above a shop is a bit like living in a caravan that's been squeezed on top of a house and is being passed off as an extension. The lines are blurred when you live above your workplace and the largest part of the home is the shop floor, which is accessible only during opening hours and which you have to share with both familiar customers and a bunch of complete strangers. Any child caught trespassing out of hours on the shop floor was either looking to nick something or had forgotten to bring in the paper stand from outside the shop. The latter was the one task you wouldn't want to forget – the paper stand could exact a fierce revenge for any delay in allowing it its respite from corner shop duty. Having spent the whole day being either peed on by dogs or used as a prop for a succession of BMX bikes, it was on guard to snap the fingers of anyone who upset it, and its metal clasps took no prisoners should it be in a bad mood. We all have the scars on our fingers to prove it.

Much like ours, Maggie's corner shop was at the end of a Victorian terrace. Fortunately for them, the Roberts girls had a room each above the shop and Maggie's overlooked the entire street, giving her a perfect vantage point of all the passers by. I too had a good position to watch the community at work and play, but I shared a room with one of my sisters while the eldest enjoyed the privacy of the top attic room. Her view took in the whole stretch of the street – including a section of electricity line that passed the window ledge on its way to a pylon station about a mile away.

This was the source of many a childhood nightmare, enhanced no doubt by the government-produced adverts that regularly warned us of the terrible dangers that a child in the 1970s and 1980s would face if they didn't heed the advice of these public information films. The 'Play Safe: Frisbee' advert was perhaps the most dark and scary of them all. Produced to warn children of the dangers of playing near pylons, the film sees young Jimmy toss his Frisbee into an electricity substation. The synthesised electronic music gathers momentum as Jimmy is encouraged by his friend to retrieve the Frisbee, which is stuck fast inside a towering steel pylon. His annoying dungaree-clad friend (the one who has told Jimmy to retrieve said Frisbee) hysterically cries his name as she, and the viewer, watches poor Jimmy's death by electrocution. I'm not sure why we had to see the graphic demise of Jimmy as the voiceover would've sufficed:

A 66,000-volt shock killed a boy today when he broke into a substation. The electricity board warns children to keep away from substations. Never try to

get toys back yourself, otherwise you may never live
to play with them again.*

And if you hadn't got the message by this point, the shrill
sound of Jimmy's friend calling his name at the point of
his death is repeated at the end.

Maggie, on the other hand, had more practical childhood worries. Her father, Alfred Roberts, ever the shrewd
businessman, deemed hot running water an unnecessary
cost, and the family lavatory was situated in the back
garden. Fortunately we did have a bathroom inside the
house, complete with sink, toilet and bath, but our
personal cross to bear was the artificial green 'grass'
carpet, an established feature of the property – which
apparently did not require any home improvement. The
polypropylene green fibres would stand to attention,
apologetically pricking your feet, as you'd try to fathom
why you were walking on the bristles of a hairbrush. It
was better than walking on nails, I suppose, but it remains
a feature of corner shop living that's forever etched in my
memory.

The details of the family accommodation, however,
pale into insignificance next to the main feature that
dominated all of our lives – the shop floor. Like my sisters
and I, Maggie spent much of her spare time working in

* Play Safe – Frisbee © Crown Copyright (1978). Reproduced with
permission of The British Film Institute under delegated authority from
the Controller of HMSO.

the shop, weighing the goods, taking orders from customers and joining her father on delivery runs.

> People would knock on the door at almost any hour of the night or weekend if they ran out of bacon, sugar, butter or eggs. Everyone knew that we lived by serving the customer; it was pointless to complain – and so nobody did.*

It may have been pointless to complain, Maggie, but we did – repeatedly. Once again I am reminded of the endless floor-mopping and the particular arguments it always raised:

1. Why do we have to do it?
2. Why do we have to do it in the dark?
3. It will only get dirty again!
4. I hate my life.

There was, I later realised, good justification for point number two (which, incidentally, placed extra strain on our young eyes as they worked overtime to scour the scene for signs of muddy activity). A shop that looked closed from the outside would dissuade any passers-by from trying their luck and walking in for that last-minute purchase at closing time, just because the lights were enticingly still on. It is these small victories that can ease the burden of corner shop life.

* *The Path to Power*, Margaret Thatcher (HarperCollins, 1995, page 15)

Sunday was the day that both Maggie's family and mine would indulge in some much-needed and precious family time. The Roberts family would typically come together for a hearty meal after they'd completed the first of their two Sunday visits to church, but the closest we'd get to any spiritual guidance would be the sounds coming from the Pentecostal church in Caversham. Its mainly black congregation would pile out of the church around midday on Sunday and if you were lucky enough to be in the vicinity at the time, you'd be witness to lavish hats, dresses in rainbow colours and plenty of smiling faces.

Unlike the Roberts, Sunday was still half a working day for our family, but that didn't stop us mirroring the Roberts' family tradition of Sunday lunch. But while they would indulge in a traditional roast dinner, our meal would take twenty-four hours to prepare and be enough to feed an army of shopkeepers and their families.

Mum would dash back and forth from the shop to the kitchen the night before to lovingly prepare the Sunday treats. The process would begin by leaving a kilogram of chickpeas to soak in water overnight before preparing a spicy tomato and onion masala sauce to smother the chickpeas in a luxurious bath before slow-cooking the whole thing for two hours. The accompaniment for the chickpea curry (cholay) would be special naan bread called a 'bhatura'. The bread is created by sheer brute force, very firmly kneading together one part maida flour and two parts water, which is then deep-fried before being served with a generous helping of tamarind sauce and a few raw onions on the side. Hey presto – the magnificent Cholay Bathura – our take on a Sunday roast. And for Dad no dish is complete without a few whole green chillies to bite into. It's a habit that even on my wedding day we indulged him in, setting them on his plate like a pair of comfy slippers in front of a tired pair of feet.

Maggie's weekend would end with a chapter or two of *Bibby's Annual* – a religious publication that was a gift from her devout Methodist parents. There was no time for bedtime reading in our house, however, as we'd usually be catching up on homework and helping out with domestic chores while Mum attempted to stay ahead of the washing and ironing as well as writing out a stock list for the next day's cash-and-carry run. Family Sundays disappeared as quickly as the British summer and, unabashed by its continued toll on family life, corner shop life would roll on regardless.

Maggie may well have daydreamed, as I did, of a different world that was free from the confines and monotony of corner shop life. We both spent years in this strange and fascinating world, our young, curious eyes taking in the sights and sounds of a community where all and sundry would walk into our home.

The corner shop provides a service to anyone willing to step through the door. A customer's class, gender, race or occupation is immaterial for those of us on the 'inside', and any judgement passed by a shopkeeper merely rests upon whether or not your wallets are full enough to make their day. This is life through the corner shop lens; a unique vantage point on the world. All of the people who walked through the doors of our shop would be oblivious to the curious eyes of the daughter of a shopkeeper carefully drinking in the words and behaviour of each customer and trying to work out what they would put in their shopping basket next. You can see why a childhood peering over the counter might lead to a career in politics.

For all the similarities between Maggie's childhood and mine, however, there is at least one distinct difference: Maggie's Britain was a very white one, as in the 1940s the corner shop was yet to encounter the Asian invasion that would soon follow. It's not as though Asian shopkeepers were responsible for the 'shop on a corner' concept – if we had been, perhaps we could have stomached the stereotypes. My mum and dad merely occupied a space that had originally been created by the finest architectural minds of post-war Britain.

The terraces of Victorian suburbia were designed as a response to the ever-increasing spread of urban communities. Town planners were put to task and we have them to thank for the two-up, two-down redbrick façades that now litter the nation. The corner shop was then an inevitability. Beautifully positioned at the junction of Britain's working-class streets, it sat – and still sits – proudly at the epicentre of suburban life. Its creation was a stroke of genius, and the Alfred Roberts of this world were quids in. Shopkeepers across the land had been given the opportunity to feed the nation from the most prominent spot in the neighbourhood. Without qualification, they were thrust into the heart of the community, happily rubbing shoulders with all classes of society.

The position of the corner shop is perfect for a thriving trade, easily attracting potential customers walking past. A savvy shopkeeper can exploit the large windows to the maximum, with colourful displays of the lush goods inside and banners detailing the latest bargains ensuring that people are lured in on sight.

A less obvious advantage for the corner shopkeeper than simple location emerged during the war, when the subsequent years of rationing meant that acquiring food to fill your empty belly could only be done at the local shop – the supermarket was yet to make its grand entrance on our shores. On 8 January 1940, bacon, butter and sugar were rationed, and several other products including meat, tea, eggs and milk soon followed. Anyone wanting to collect their food allowance had to register in their local shop, as it was the only way you could get your hands on the slim pickings.

In 1940s Britain, living costs had trebled and with rising fuel prices customers were unlikely to venture further afield for the daily or weekly shop, even if they'd had the option. But familiarity breeds benefits, and if things were a struggle, and you had been smart enough to stay on friendly terms with the Mr Roberts of this world, there was a solution to the financial constraints of a family shopping list. Enter stage right – our dutiful shopkeeper with his honourable shopping solution: Groceries 'on tick'.

A blessing for the customer – and sometimes a curse for the shopkeeper – 'on tick' was a business arrangement based entirely on trust. Shopkeepers would make a judgement on the customer's promise that they would return to pay for their goods sometime in the near future. For some this was a way of life and shopkeepers had to strike a careful balance between credit control and offending the clientele. Just as an animal is branded at market, a customer's name was highlighted until the debt was settled with a ✓. Decades later Mum and Dad offered this service with questionable success, as the animals would often run wild.

Fully established as a must-have for every community, the corner shop set precedents between shopkeeper and customer. A relationship based on convenience, patience and conviviality was born, and for the length of a visit, economic woes and personal hardship were temporarily forgotten. It was a place to meet familiar faces and help people out. It also provided buckets of entertainment in a world that had not yet embraced television. The corner shop became a nerve centre of information and regular visitors would choose to divulge or absorb the goings-on in their street. The tin cans would rattle with the mutterings of this newly formed gossip hub.

The corner shop was the butcher, the baker and the

candlestick maker. It was also the Florence Nightingale of a country that was yet to be blessed by Aneurin Bevan's National Health Service. As my parents often proclaim, the NHS is the single most important contribution to British society, and what has made this country great. True advocates of the service, Mum and Dad believe that any system that offers state-sponsored care for every individual is to be celebrated, respected and cherished. Their GP is almost god-like in their eyes. Even when Mum was misdiagnosed when suffering from pneumonia in her seventies, we were still unable to say a bad word about the doctor in her company.

Before the introduction of the NHS, Britain's parents were reliant on corner shop suggestions to keep illnesses at bay. Children would be subjected to a weekly dose of liquid paraffin or syrup of figs to keep the bowels moving – all available at your friendly trusted local shop, of course. In later years this 'anything you need' service was perfected by Asian shopkeepers, who would guarantee a year-round supply of Christmas decorations or an open all hours culture that was unrivalled and, for your custom, a bag of fizzy cola bottles to ensure you'll pop by again.

Before the 1950s, corner shop culture was all about one-to-one time with the shopkeeper. There was no opportunity to examine your goods before buying. The shop counter and its keeper remained the prime obstacle you had to navigate before you could lay your hands on any of its offerings. The customer had to perfect a peer-and-point tactic and once you reached the point of service, those waiting in line would learn much about your life, including whether you had any financial woes.

The shopkeeper loomed large behind the counter. You'd have to rattle off your list to an uninvited audience of nosy shoppers. If you tried to be discreet, the 'collect and pack' stage would out you. Shopping had to take place most days because, with no fridges at home, there was nowhere to store perishable goods. Customers would bump into each other regularly and chat away about the goings-on in their street. There was no escape and from start to finish this most mundane of activities could take up to an hour.

But more fool you if you tried to rush it, as any item missed on your shopping list would have to abide by the rules of opening times. Trade operated by way of a sociable hour. On Saturdays most corner shops were shut by midday and you'd have to wait until Monday if you'd forgotten something. It would have been useful to point this out to Mum and Dad, because operational hours and trading laws clearly passed them by. The next generation of Britain's shopkeepers had no idea about the corner shop etiquette that had gone before.

The corner shop held a prominent role as the provider of all family needs. It was also the golden age for the shopkeeper who reigned supreme as the master of consumer goods. But a shopping revolution was around the corner. Post-war Britain was moving forward and she was ready to loosen the restrictions imposed by the now-receding war. The little corner shop was about to face its first big threat and enter into a David and Goliath battle that would last for decades.

4

Americana

'Give your customers the stuff they want, but also the stuff they don't know they want.'
Shopkeeper Rule No1, Secret Code (date unknown)

In 1953 a newly qualified barrister and now mum of twins, Margaret Thatcher, was dipping her toe into British politics just as a transatlantic phenomenon arrived to bulldoze the corner shops of her childhood into near obscurity.

Rationing officially ended in 1954, and over the next decade a dramatic rise in the standard of living and a boom in the British economy meant that Britons were shaking off the shackles of post-war austerity and on a quest for freedom and a new identity. So what better time for the USA, which had emerged after the Second World War as the dominant global power, to promote its cultural influence? American music, cinema and television filtered into British life at a time when people were more affluent and their spending power was on the up. American ideas were impacting on mainstream society, and consumerism was leading the way.

The protection of the consumer's interests had always been part of corner shop life. We were the ones that nurtured the bond between shopkeeper and customer. We were the ones that lovingly ordered the forehock to be carefully cut up and sliced ready for collection at 9 a.m. We were the ones that guarded scarce commodities during the war and we were the ones that kept secret a customer's marital woes or financial crises. But the corner shop and its position in British society were about to be discarded like a pair of old dust sheets, thanks to a new-found love for Americana and the emergence of large self-service shops selling food and household goods. All hail the arrival of the supermarket – America's precocious new offspring.

The supermarket arrived in Britain in perfect synchronicity with the nation's newly acquired consumerism. It coincided with the country's aspirational needs and marked the start of an era of mass consumption that continues to this day. In his essay 'The Americanization of the European Economy', Harm G. Schröter remarked, 'this bedevilled "triumphal march of self service" holds us in its claws'*.

Premiers Supermarkets opened the very first self-service store in Streatham, London in 1951 and soon the country was littered with other American-style supermarkets. Like rabbits at Easter time, supermarkets sprung up all over the

---

* *Americanization of the European Economy*, Harm G. Schröter (Springer, 2005)

nation and by 1956 there were three thousand supermarkets in operation,* with Tesco, Safeway, and Sainsbury's becoming household names. The gleaming displays of mass consumerism and cheap prices were paraded like a pair of silk stockings. They turned our heads. Giddy with excitement, the nation's shoppers were tripping over each other to get inside these new temples of merchandise.

Typically the American invaders would stake out a space covering 2,000 square feet. Here you could walk, run or waltz your way through the aisles. There was no need to peer over a counter at your goods or to ask the shopkeeper, dressed in strange white overalls, to pass you a loaf of bread. You could peruse the aisles, pick an item off the shelf and put it directly into the shopping basket you picked up on your way in. This was a shopping revolution.

The supermarket had gatecrashed its way into British life at the perfect time. With more women at work, the once-daily trip to the corner shop was replaced by a far more manageable weekly excursion to the supermarket. And once inside, it was all about customer appeal. The tins of prunes and spam no longer had to court the shopper from behind a counter looking for a satisfactory glance of approval. The time had come for the consumer to step up to centre stage and enjoy a new array of goodies that shamelessly paraded themselves for the taking.

* 'The Rise and Fall of the Corner Shop', Seren Charrington-Hollins, February 2015

The scale of the supermarket left the corner shop's mouth ajar. Each aisle was stacked high with the promise of a new experience. Brightly coloured packaging showing white children with broad smiles covered American products such as Colgate toothpaste, or breakfast cereals that would induce a sugar frenzy among the little darlings who could be seen bouncing around the aisles full of Crosse & Blackwell baked beans and Fairy Liquid. Praise must go to the geniuses who wrote the famous advertising jingle for the latter: 'Now hands that do dishes can be as soft as your face with mild green Fairy Liquid', which helped the Fairy Liquid brand dominate the washing up liquid market. Self-service was all about advertising and brand packaging, and Britons couldn't get enough of it.

Products had to sell themselves and convince you to lift them off a perfectly positioned shelf – it was a far cry from being separated from the products in the local corner shop. By the sixties, your eyes might align seamlessly with Paul, John, Ringo and George, whose faces were plastered across a box of Beatles Bars: 'four delicious ice cream bars covered with chocolate crunch'. This product exploited the 'best of British', but was manufactured in the USA to be exported back to Britain, all the while making the supermarkets and the ice-cream manufacturers in New Jersey a tidy profit.

Refrigeration, dehydration and transportation were the other great American exports that were revolutionising domestic life in the early sixties. The working class was now able to take advantage of affordable luxury goods that had previously been out of reach. With increased spending power, many more people were also able to buy cars, allowing them a new sense of freedom with day trips and weekend excursions away from the confines of home. Consumption was no longer about a utilitarian need, as defined by the corner shop. This was about status and comfort, and the Americans were success-fully feeding off a change in Britain's social and working habits.

For some, the Americanisation of British culture signi-fied the degradation of society and a loss of traditional British values. But for young Britons, in particular, America was fun and exciting. Suddenly the 'you've never had it so good' affluence was reaching working-class neighbourhoods that were enjoying the freedom to choose their identity through popular culture, mass media and fashion. A nation hooked on Hollywood films bought into the cult figure epitomised by actor James Dean in the movie *Rebel Without a Cause*. Here was Jim Stark (Dean), at odds with his parents' generation, who were failing to understand teenage angst. Britain lapped it up as Hollywood spoon-fed us Americana in much the same way as its self-service stores did.

And just to make sure you wouldn't return to old shop-ping habits, customers were rewarded for their loyalty to supermarkets with trading stamps, another gift from our allies across the pond. The more money you spent in store, the more stamps you'd collect, which could then be exchanged for gifts chosen from a Green Shield Stamps catalogue. The stamps were incredibly popular and the supermarkets battled it out over who could offer the customer double or triple reward stamps. The founder of Tesco, Sir Jack Cohen, signed his store up to a Green Shield Stamps scheme in the 1960s. It was a brilliant tie-in and helped to establish Tesco as a future giant in Britain's retail industry.

It was a clever ruse – the customer felt he or she was getting something for nothing, when in fact consumers were paying sixpence for every stamp collected. One single book alone required a full set of 1,280 stamps before you could move up the ladder of a catalogue of dreams to collect a 'luxury' item. It's the stamps you can thank for your grandparents' or parents' dodgy Formica kitchenware, or the ironing boards that collapse into a heap at your feet with the minimal amount of pressure.

And what was going on outside the supermarket was just as important as its glossy interior. A parking space alone would invite the widest customer grin of all. Each space was carefully marked out in white or yellow lines and was spacious by design, so much so that it seems our American friends may have presumed the British public were driving Cadillacs measuring 6 metres from bonnet to boot.

The simple trolley-to-car experience had small businesses and shopkeepers hanging their heads in despair. The modern superstore on the edge of town, surrounded by free parking spaces and selling a huge range of low-cost produce, was irresistible. Customers now roamed free and for them the newly found independence was liberating. No longer worried about the prying eyes of a shopkeeper, the shopping trip became a fun and personal experience without fear of judgement. There was no need to spend hours queuing up among the big ears of the neighbourhood who could hear your shopping order and derive from it the apparent personal goings-on in your home. The supermarket did away with corner shop etiquette and the customer could now buy what they wanted, when they wanted it.

Britain was stuck in a supermarket coma. By 1960 the average supermarket was making at least ten times more than the general stores and there were 12,000 in operation.* The supermarket offered what the corner shop could not – glamour, privacy, choice and freedom – and there was no way the shopkeeper could fathom to keep up. We were totally in love with the beauty of it all and any reminiscing about the corner shop tradition became rare – a convenient weekly shop with the customer in charge was being celebrated across the country. Between 1956 and 1960, the number of general stores fell by 56.2 per cent.† To make matters worse, the key thing independent traders relied upon was soon snatched away.

---

* From 'Food Stories', Retail Experience, hosted by the British Library (www.bl.uk/learning/citizenship/foodstories/Accessible/retailingexperience/retailexperienceintro.html)
† *The Changing Geography of the UK 3rd Edition*, Hugh Matthews and Vince Gardiner (ed.) (Routledge, 1999)

There was one factor that kept the corner shop on the same platform as larger traders – Resale Price Maintenance (RPM). RPM obliged shops to sell goods at a standard price set by suppliers, which prevented big businesses from using the brutal tactic of undercutting. But in 1964 the House of Commons passed a law to abolish RPM, which opened the floodgates of competition and gave the supermarkets ample opportunity to expand and transform the retail landscape of Britain.

Bereft and stripped of its assets, the corner shop, once the champion of the community, became a pitiful sight across Britain. Unable to compete with the big boys, the spot on the corner resembled a neglected brothel with no make-up or frilly knickers to entice the customers.

The supermarket and its vast array of shiny, brightly coloured products was a smooth operator, a subtle invader that crept in under the door as we slowly fell in love with an American capitalist system and its way of life. Father Christmas swigging on a bottle of Coca-Cola symbolises the peak of Britain's mass consumption of Americana. The Coca-Cola Santa became a celebrated feature of Christmas and appeared in newspapers, on billboards and in TV advertisements across the world. We all apparently needed a few bottles of Coca-Cola in our great big fridges because Santa told us so. It was his beverage of choice as he delivered presents in his one-horse open sleigh.

Mass consumption did its bit to serve the tastes of the British consumer who absorbed the American ideals of consumerism and aspiration to wealth. The supermarket had stolen rule number one from the corner shop bible: give the customer what they think they need as well as what they want. A rule that was reclaimed a decade later by a new generation of shopkeeper.

By 1968, 50 per cent of households were the proud owners of a bulky, space-hogging refrigerator* and busy mums stocked it with a variety of supermarket-supplied fresh food in novel polythene packaging. And thanks to a bunch of food chemists and the technique of gas chromatography (which identifies aroma compounds of different ingredients), artificial flavourings led to the creation of products such as Dream Topping (a substitute for whipped cream) and prawn cocktail flavoured crisps. Dehydrated foods were also a welcome quick fix for an evening meal – Smash, for example, consisted of granulated pieces of potato stuffed into a large sachet. The ads for this product would later become some of the most iconic of my youth: the vigorous 'For Mash Get Smash' campaign left an image of a Martian preparing mashed potato firmly etched into the minds of children who grew up in the late 1970s and 1980s.

So from the sixties onwards, the old corner shop model of shopping was on its last legs and had become as parochial and outdated as its masters. It had stocked up and served up when the nation asked it to, but it saw no point in

* 'The Rise and Transformation of the UK Domestic Appliances Industry', Huw Beynon, Surhan Cam, Peter Fairbrother and Theo Nichols (School of Social Sciences Working Papers Series, vol. 42. Cardiff University, October 2003)

fighting on. The struggle was too much for thousands of white working-class shopkeepers, who decided to shut up shop and call time on the spot that was once the cornerstone of the community.

Where were you, Britain, to salvage that tiny spot on the corner that breathed life into a community? Where were you to help the underdog in its hour of need? Well, what the corner shop couldn't accomplish by steadily plodding on it would have to achieve by finding a new direction. With its own exotic identity and fashion sense, a superhero was coming to the rescue.

We do have a lot to thank 'the immigrants' for, including:

- Rebuilding the spine of a nation by enabling Britain to kick away its post-war crutches and flourish in textiles and manufacturing, thanks to the influx of immigrants in the late 1950s and 1960s.
- Getting us safely from A to B, thanks to thousands of workers from the Caribbean who first arrived here in 1948 and continued to man the nation's trains, buses, tubes and waterways.
- Keeping us from our deathbeds when thousands of nurses and doctors arrived from overseas to fill a job shortage caused by NHS expansion in the 1950s.

But in a way it is the corner shop that probably owes the biggest debt to the immigrant for breathing life back into its rusting shelves and repairing its broken dreams.

Despite Goliath kicking the shit out of David, the corner shop was not completely brought to its knees by the supermarket, which had little time or inclination to notice that its smaller rival still had a weapon in its armoury. The weapon, however, was not easy to spot until a new generation of shopkeepers decided to walk among the shards of forgotten memories with the hope of re-inventing this little kingdom once more. The supermarket, for all its big balls and its hype, was far too busy congrat-ulating itself to appreciate the secret to corner shop rein-vention. It failed to recognise that its adversary, whom it had ruled out as viable competition, possessed an essen-tial attribute for retail success: the ability to respond to an emergency.

Families were reeled in to the unique experience of supermarket shopping by heading to the outskirts of Britain's large urban communities where most of the country's supermarkets had set up shop. A weekly excur-sion where all the family would pile into the car for an enjoyable day out was still very much a novel experience. Yet the shopping adventure failed to factor in that every community still needed somewhere close to home for their last-minute 'I've run out of sugar and I can't stand my neighbour' shopping essentials.

Yes, the corner shop was small; no, it didn't look as swanky as a supermarket, but here was a space free of metal turnstiles bashing into your hips, or multiple aisles of confusion. The corner shop was not a hindrance but an accelerator for your grab-and-go bag of sugar. This item and dozens like it could be bought at any time without causing a dip in your fuel tank; it required no more than a few steps down the road – in your slippers if you chose – and a shopkeeper's helpful direction to unite you with a much-needed bag of Tate & Lyle. The emergency moments are what the corner shop lives for. It has a track record of serving a nation at the most desperate of times and there is no way the supermarket can take that away from it.

The self-service shops hadn't accounted for the forgetfulness of the British shopper either. The missed items on a shopping list can cause great anxiety for the customer, but it's a stress that can be alleviated within minutes courtesy of the little shop on the corner. It's one thing to have a fridge fully stocked with ready meals, but to upset Grandma by forgetting to get a card for her birthday tomorrow is an unimaginable disaster.

The supermarket failed to recognise the fact that before it arrived on the block, the nation had relied on the humble corner shop during times of personal crisis. Dynasties of shopkeepers had sold to dynasties of customers and they had known one another from cradle to grave. The big players have, to this day, been unable to replicate the unique shopkeeper–customer relationship, and they'd do well to remember that this special bond doesn't happen overnight but is something that is built over time.

The law regarding trading hours was also on the corner shop's side, giving us another advantage over Big Brother. The 1950 Shops Act had imposed rigid controls on when conventional stores, including supermarkets, could be open, and the law enforcers were predominantly concerned with the supermarkets, who could potentially fall foul of the law in a very public way. The tiny battered spaces on Britain's street corners were not worth the hassle of litigation at the taxpayers' expense and shopkeepers knew it. The daring among them could easily extend trading hours without fear of prosecution.

Despite the power of the supermarkets, then, the corner shop was still a potentially viable business model with some advantages over its bigger rival. Yet to take on the supermarkets was considered foolish by a generation of white British corner shop owners, who had had first-hand experience of running a shop in the face of overwhelming competition. To many, the challenges appeared insurmountable, and there was no guarantee that the corner shop could ever occupy a prominent space in British life again.

But to others it seemed worth a shot. The time had come to shake off the dustsheets and reinvent this little space with an army of willing volunteers. The idea of reviving the fortunes of the corner shop spread like wildfire across Britain's factory floors, for it was here that the next generation of shopkeepers could be found. Young and full of boundless energy, the immigrants of Britain were willing to take on the forgotten child of a nation and navigate her through the uncharted waters of opening all hours and Sunday trading. There was an unspoken internal mantra in Britain's newly formed immigrant communities that I imagine went a bit like this:

'There is a place that glistens under UV lights. A place where every penny spent is two more in your pocket. A place you can call home and a place where you will be the master.'

In reality it was more ordinary. One uncleji speaks to another and then heads home after a fourteen-hour day in the factory where he chats to his biological uncleji (with whom he lives) who then talks to his wife to seek approval (which she gives) and an idea gathers momentum and crucially, financial backing.

The mantra becomes a reality:

'There's a shop on the corner . . . it's all boarded up. Sanj took it over and bought it really cheap and it's doing okay. If we get some cash together maybe we can take it on . . . What d'you reckon?'

However it happened, the opportunity to work for yourself was sent from heaven for the Asian factory worker who was fed up of working his or her backside off for a pittance. And the now-destitute corner shop was ripe for a change in fortune.

It seems that the Alfred Roberts of this world weren't aware of the whisperings among the Asian communities of Britain. Maggie's father sold his shop in 1958 and settled for a life preaching in the local church and as an active member of the Rotary Club. Had there been more conversation between the old guard and the new, a secret of the potential prosperous times ahead for the corner shop could have been shared that might have rescued a whole generation of shopkeepers who had served the country well. But their downfall was rich pickings for thousands of immigrants, who were about to change the face of Britain's streets forever.

5

Love Thy Neighbour

'Do unto others as you would have them do unto you, otherwise they'll charge lower prices and nick your customers.'
Shopkeeper banter, cash & carry car park, Reading

The corner shop was about to become a rite of passage and a route to independence for thousands of immigrants who, like my father, were tired of the unrewarding factory floor. It presented an opportunity. Take up the role of master and be guaranteed to line your own pockets for once, and to operate without a chain of command. A one-boss mandate where the shopkeeper could do whatever he or she wanted was seen as the ticket to freedom.

Within a few years of the Indian community starting to take over these little shops, the highly skilled professionals from East Africa who had been banished from their homes like vermin also began taking up the mantle as some of the UK's finest corner shop proprietors. There was no hiding the deep suspicion from the Indians who by this stage were well on their way to domineering the corner shop market. The East African Asians, with their entrepreneurial guile and beautiful features, had also cottoned on to the secret potential of the corner shop. Reinventing themselves and the corner shops of Britain may well have been seen as an insurmountable challenge, but Indians had already paved the way with moderate success and, with gusto and self-belief, anything was possible.

However, every Asian immigrant who'd entered the UK, whether they'd been expelled or whether they'd been given an employment voucher and fifty quid to come here, had a common goal: to succeed at any cost. With every foreigner that walked off the plane, a new work ethic grew. Under no circumstances would any member of this community accept a hand-out. We were, as it turns out, too proud to beg, and competition for corner shop leases became fierce.

The subject of state welfare did, in fact, provoke much lively family discussion on any given Saturday night. The men in our family would indulge in a whisky and 'roti' (dinner) session that lasted into the small hours of the night, and emboldened by the devil's drink, they'd dissect the state of country and customer relations on the shop floor. The idea that a government was willing to pay you for doing nothing was the cause for much belly laughter during their boozy sessions. Signing on to collect so-called 'dole money' completely dumbfounded my uncle (one of the biological ones in this case). In Laurel and Hardy fashion, he would slap his forehead with exasperation and roll around the sofa in a fit of hysteria, predicting a future full of fraudulent time-wasters spreading like the common cold.

Welfare was never an option for us. There'd be nothing worse than to be spotted standing in the dole queue on a Monday afternoon and being at the centre of the gossip mill. It was one thing to arrive in this country penniless, but pride ensured such an existence would be a temporary one. The work ethic of the East African Asian community revealed that they clearly felt the same.

But as the government found itself facing difficult times at home and abroad, an immigration policy that was deemed by some to be too 'open door' was beginning to create ripples of distrust. The far right National Front (NF) was founded in 1967. It capitalised on the growing concern regarding Asian migration to Britain, and membership applications to the group rocketed. The NF labelled itself as a racial nationalist party, opposing all coloured immigration to Britain and advocating the repatriation of all immigrants who had made the country their home. The group brilliantly exploited the climate of fear infecting the UK, and its public profile was boosted through demonstrations, rallies and marches in parts of London and the north of England. Far right groups were gaining traction and a mantra of 'white jobs for white people' was heard on many inner-city streets. It also made it to the doorsteps of the country's corner shops now in the hands of immigrant families.

However, racial divisions were clearly forgotten when groceries and other supplies were required. My uncle (biological, twice removed on my mum's side) recalls how the NF boys came to their shop to stock up on supplies of crisps, beer and fags before heading out to march on the streets of Derby. One man in particular, called Dom, had always been on friendly terms with my uncle, but now at the age of twenty-one his membership of the National Front was clearly causing him inner conflict. Should he ignore the immigrant shopkeeper that he had known since he was a child? The angst on Dom's face was clearly visible as he and his NF mates gathered outside the shop, swigging cans of Diamond White and intimidating the customers. My uncle was surprisingly sympathetic about Dom's predicament, and, despite avoiding all eye contact with my uncle, Dom and his mates were never barred from entering the shop. For years their strange relationship continued in this way. It was as if they both understood that Dom's allegiance to a racist political party was more about bravado than a deep-seated ideological belief. Besides, corner shop custom dictates that your money is good no matter what your political or social status. You can be a racist as long as it's our shop you spend your cash in.

As far as the racists were concerned, distinctions within Asian communities were entirely blurred. It didn't matter that Mr Patel was originally from Gujarat, had migrated to Uganda and was now a refugee in Britain, and a devout Hindu and teetotal vegetarian. Nor did it matter that Dad, who was invited here, made the best chicken curry in the world, smoked Rothmans Blue and as a Punjabi was almost duty-bound to regularly sample a glass or two of Johnny Walker (or as my aunt called it, 'Walking Black Johnny'). We were all brown. Simple.

At least Idi Amin was more creative with his labelling; 'bloodsucker' sounds punchier than 'brown'. But to be reduced to just a colour and a faceless, nameless one at that, was perhaps the most soul-destroying thing you could do to a person. To this day it's the one thing I have been unable to get my head round. Was 'brown' all the customers ever saw when they looked at us and exchanged pleasantries with us over the shop counter?

A stark warning was issued in the UK on 20 April 1968 that apparently our rivers would soon flow with scarlet blood, the kind that only came from immigrants. Immigrants like us: the coloured variety.

Maybe Enoch Powell knew something the rest of us didn't when he delivered his Rivers of Blood speech to members of the Conservative Party in Birmingham in 1968. Before he crawled into bed on the eve of the speech, perhaps his own bedtime ritual inspired him. Maybe, as he parted each thinning strand of grey with a wide-toothed comb, watching the hair fall mercilessly away from his thinning crown, he had an epiphany:

'I warn you now.
The bloodsuckers are coming.

Demons possessed, they will use their own blood to violently vomit infection into the rivers of Great Britain.'

Enoch Powell tapped into the fear that was sweeping across Britain and became the poster boy for the far right movement. Although he was briefly admonished by the Conservative Party for his racist speech, he gained support from the corners of Britain that felt marginalised and overwhelmed by the invasion of black and brown faces.

Powell's main gripe was the Race Relations Act of 1968, which prohibits discrimination on the grounds of race. The act made it illegal to refuse housing, employment or public services to a person on the basis of colour, race, ethnic or national origins. It also created the Community Relations Commission, which was supposed to promote 'harmonious community relations'. Powell did not like this in the slightest, especially if it meant coloured folks were given preference for housing over their white counterparts.

Unfortunately, his words seemed to strike a chord. A Gallup poll taken at the end of April 1968 showed that 74 per cent of respondents agreed with his speech and 69 per cent thought Edward Heath was wrong to have sacked him. The Rivers of Blood speech turned the Wolverhampton MP into a national figure. Mum and Dad and our extended family were now lumped together with tens of thousands of black and Asian immigrants and publicly outed as the 'alien'.

For the first time since the 1930s the number of people out of work and claiming benefits had risen above one million. The then chancellor, Anthony Barber, proposed a number of measures to help boost the economy and get people back to work. In his 1972 budget, he ambitiously announced to Parliament that he would add 10 per cent to the UK's growth in two years and, despite more than three billion in public sector borrowing required, Chancellor Barber claimed he would be able to reduce income taxes by a billion pounds and offer huge tax concessions to industry in order to save jobs. He failed. Inflation soared and within months he was forced to bring in a deflationary budget and a pay freeze that led to a major confrontation with the miners. The mood of the nation was turning sour, and by 1972 and at the height of immigration from Commonwealth countries into Britain, the blame game was well and truly under-way. A country that had once begged for foreign help was split on the value of immigration. The debate became a racial one.

Subtle and not-so-subtle racism soon became the norm. Many entering into the corner shop trade were willing to turn a blind eye to it, but it wasn't easy. Enoch Powell had blurred the lines of what people could and couldn't say. This Savile Row-suited, white, middle-class professor with a double first from Cambridge and a steely moustache put a legitimate face on being racist. He gave the green light to far right groups to act hostilely towards a group of people – us.

TV footage and audio recordings of Powell's speech are incomplete, but there are countless voiceover recordings in existence of the exact words he used on that grey day in Birmingham. I had never listened to or read the full Rivers of Blood speech until 1994, when a college friend invited me to listen to a dubbed version on his Sony Walkman. Delightfully sandwiched between a playlist of Jodeci and the Beastie Boys was Powell's every racist word.

'As time goes on, the proportion of this total who are immigrant descendants, those born in England, who arrived here by exactly the same route as the rest of us, will rapidly increase. Already by 1985, the native-born would constitute the majority. It is this fact which creates the extreme urgency of action now, of just that kind of action which is hardest for politicians to take, action where the difficulties lie in the present but the evils to be prevented or minimised lie several parliaments ahead.

The natural and rational first question with a nation confronted by such a prospect is to ask: "How can its dimensions be reduced?" Granted it be not wholly preventable, can it be limited, bearing in mind that numbers are of the essence: the significance and consequences of an alien element introduced into a country or population are profoundly different according to whether that element is 1 per cent or 10 per cent.

The answers to the simple and rational question are equally simple and rational: by stopping, or virtually stopping, further inflow, and by promoting the maximum outflow. Both answers are part of the official policy of the Conservative Party.

It almost passes belief that at this moment twenty or thirty additional immigrant children are arriving from overseas in Wolverhampton alone every week – and that means fifteen or twenty additional families a decade or two hence. Those whom the gods wish to destroy, they first make mad. We must be mad, literally mad, as a nation to be permitting the annual inflow of some 50,000 dependants, who are for the most part the material of the future growth of the immigrant-descended population. It is like watching a nation busily engaged in heaping up its own funeral pyre. So insane are we that we actually permit unmarried persons to immigrate for the purpose of founding a family with spouses and fiancés whom they have never seen.'*

Powell's prophetic powers predicted that by the year 2000, around 7 million people living in the UK would be of ethnic descent. In actual fact the 2001 census revealed that 4.6 million were considered to be from an ethnic minority (around 7.9 per cent of the population).

* Parliamentary material licensed under the Open Parliament Licence v.30.

I felt as British as the Sherbet Lemons we sold in the very British institution of our corner shop. But listening to Powell, I felt as though even my breathing could potentially taint the motherland.

I am being told off for my existence.

I am jeopardising the future of Great Britain.

I am bad.

I am a wide-grinning piccaninny . . . apparently.

The latter term was a new one for me, but when I discovered the meaning of Powell's derogatory phrase I was disgusted. My parents, however, had no time for my moral outrage: they knew all too well how Britain could turn on them, despite the sweat and tears they had contributed to its survival. They had had more than two decades to digest it and didn't much care for their disgruntled teenage daughter stirring up memories more than twenty years too late. A conversation about the speech was quickly thwarted by an order to sweep the stairs. The household chores of a corner shop family will always take precedence over a *Question Time*-style debate. When there's a job to be done, time will wait for no man, not even Enoch Powell.

I was perplexed as to why I was the one in the family who was regularly tasked with the stair-clean, which was one of the biggest pains in the backside. It was a dustpan and brush job, which required much effort to be put into a tiresome and fiddly task. Each step required precision sweeping, which would begin with your brush-holding hand contorting into a right angle to reach the upright side of each step before you felt able to move on to the next level. My eyes would grow tired and sore as I'd struggle to differentiate between a speck of dirt and the hues of red and brown on the psychedelic patterned carpet. It wasn't just Powell that was giving me a headache. It was forty-five minutes out of my day that I could've spent lamenting the political situation with Dad.

The River Thames was an unremarkable muddy green colour, often littered with used joints and fag ends and always strewn with rubbish. It was the river I knew, growing up, and it did not, as far as I could see, ever run blood red. Some eight years after Enoch Powell's speech, however, a Nazi dagger was found in the River Thames. The sheathed dagger was inscribed with 'ALLES FÜR DEUTSCHLAND' in gothic lettering along the blade and featured a lightning bolt with an arrow symbol on the outer case representing Hitler's paramilitary organisation, the SA. How it got into the Thames remains a mystery. Many theories suggest it could have been dropped from a German aircraft or that it was brought in from Europe by an English solider who later discarded it into the river, disgusted by its link to the Hitler regime. Whatever the truth, it served as a reminder of how difficult it is to forget the dark chapters in our history. And thanks to Enoch Powell, 'them and us' culture became an integral element of Britain's emerging multi-cultural society.

Just like the changing faces of the corner shop, there

would be plenty of versions of Enoch Powell to come. In a climate of the 'other', the invaluable contribution made by tens of thousands of immigrants to British life went largely unnoticed. The gloves were off and the immigration debate would remain a point of contention into the next millennium.

Mind you, in the mid-1970s, with milk at 11p a pint and bread at 15p a loaf, the corner shop industry was on the up. And our customers could be seen queuing round the corner, lining up to spend their dosh in our little empire. So much for your rivers of blood, Enoch – not a drop was shed. Business was booming.

6

A Nation of Shopkeepers

'Be your own boss. Call the shots. Count the jammy dodgers and play nicely.'

Mum, 1988

Napoleon Bonaparte is often quoted as having sneeringly described the British as 'a nation of shopkeepers' – he thought the British were unfit for war, allegedly too concerned with commerce to be a credible opponent for his French army. In fact, the quote was stolen from Adam Smith, the eighteenth-century father of modern British economics and one-time inspiration for Margaret Thatcher, whose own story intersects so frequently with that of the corner shop.

My family's personal corner shop story began in 1977, when Mum and Dad became the proud owners of their first corner shop in Reading, Berkshire. In the year of Queen Elizabeth II's Silver Jubilee the country was trying to work out its relationship with immigrants, who were still arriving in their thousands. It was something that my

folks were paying little attention to, as they were preoccupied with the expansion of their family from four to
five, and I was born in the Royal Berkshire Hospital on 23
April. The nurses informed Mum it was auspicious to be
born on St George's Day, but after two days in labour,
Mum cared little that her new daughter shared a day with
the patron saint of England. Nor was she aware of the
clash that same afternoon between a thousand National
Front members and anti-fascist protestors at Duckett's
Common in London.

The soundtrack of my birth year was the Sex Pistols'
'God Save the Queen'. It mocked the government and
became the anthem for a disenchanted working-class youth.
With another year of double-digit inflation came high unemployment and slow growth. A once proud industrial base
was crumbling and people were at the mercy of union leaders for jobs. Power cuts were standard and industries were
confined to a three-day working week to conserve energy. It
wasn't looking good for Dad, as an immigrant factory
worker, nor for many of his contemporaries.

Against this bleak backdrop the newly built M4
motorway running from London to South Wales
offered a number of opportunities at its many junc-
tions. By the early 1970s Slough was spilling over with
new immigrants, but the expanding Great Western
mainline railway was pushing Reading into a new era.
It had become a popular choice with its low house
prices and close proximity to the capital, and Mum
and Dad could smell its promise in the air. The

majority of the Mars workforce lived along the M4 corridor and, like many other employees, Dad made use of the free coach service supplied by the company to ensure a happy and punctual workforce. Reading was one of the stops – far enough to escape extended family, but close enough for the compulsory weekend visits (Asian custom means you are obliged to play happy families).

Anyone from this part of the world will be familiar with Reading's cemetery junction, where the roads converge at a cemetery dating back to 1842. One of the most recognisable parts of Reading, it's also a major bottleneck, the gateway for immigration into the city, and the spot where Mum and Dad would set down temporary roots as corner shop proprietors. The wider city became their home for the next fifty years and it's where they still live, albeit in a more comfortable setting than above a corner shop.

For many immigrants, the corner shop was the pinnacle of working life. Make money and be your own boss. They didn't want to be booted off the factory floor when the country was in economic crisis. And it was in crisis. By the mid-1970s, like Greece and Cyprus in more recent times, Britain had to be bailed out by the International Monetary Fund to the tune of some four billion dollars. Desperately seeking help from our European neighbours to counter our weak pound and prop up our flailing economy was the only way to prevent the country from going bust.

So, after an extended family meeting, Reading was deemed the ideal spot for a new entrepreneurial venture for a full-time working mum of three. The beauty of the corner shop, Mum was told, was that it provided a living space that transformed into a working one. The theory was that when the bell rang signalling the arrival of a customer, Mum would be able to leave me, a newborn baby, in the back of the shop for as long as it took to serve a customer before returning to mothering duties.

The work/life 'balance' was never achieved but at least we were in good company. Young immigrant families, who had come to the UK to provide a better life for themselves, had their eyes firmly on the prize. Creating a better future for their children was the reason the shop was allowed to dominate family life. It became the big brother we never had. It almost felt like a protective blanket that was there to support us no matter how trying times might be. And it generated an income that gave us food, shelter and the ability to save for a future with hope of advancing the family's lot in life.

Mum and Dad's initial foray into the corner shop world involved taking over a business that was disappointingly unassuming. The small grocery store had previously been in the hands of an English couple for more than fifty years, and by the time Mum and Dad got their hands on it, it was pretty much on its last legs. It had been starved of love and attention, and was a prime example of what had gone so wrong with the corner shops of Britain. Most people would have walked straight past the drab spot, but Mum and Dad were positively thrilled about taking over the cracked ceilings and soiled floors.

Dad had first spotted that a shop was up for sale in *Daltons Weekly*, a national newspaper that enjoyed a healthy readership and had become a must-read for Asians who were looking for hidden treasures among the thousands of adverts of businesses for sale. The previous owners dragged their heels during the selling process almost as much as they had dragged the business into the doldrums. Mum recalls thinking at one point that they'd never get the dream they had hoped for. It is of course worth reminding her that you should be careful what you wish for. After eight months of waiting, however, in September 1977 they finally signed on the dotted line and became fully fledged corner shop owners.

When they moved in, Dad couldn't believe a shop in such a state of disrepair was still able to trade. Mum was more comforted by the repeated 'ker-ching' ringing out from the till and the influx of customers who seemed undaunted by the shop's dilapidated shell. Perhaps it was like a public toilet in that respect: unappealing as it might appear, when you needed to go, you needed to go, and so despite its state of neglect, the corner shop continued to hold its own.

Buying the shop was buying into a way of life. Naturally the property included the living quarters above the shop:

three small bedrooms and a bathroom, which, like the shop, resembled not much more than a disused shack. But like any young, enthusiastic entrepreneurs, Mum and Dad refused to be overcome by the challenging circumstances, and with plenty of elbow grease and a sense of humour, the shop quickly became unrecognizable.

There was one significant issue, however. The previous owners had refused to move with the times and had managed to get away without acquiring a fridge for perishable goods. Mum quizzed the previous owners about where they had stored the milk, butter and cheese. They casually remarked that a draught had adequately preserved any items placed near the front door. They were defiant; a refrigerator was not required.

In the fifty years that the couple had operated as shopkeepers, not once were they inspected by officials from the health and safety department. Yet within two days of reopening the shop, Mum and Dad received a visit. The ageing, stocky health and safety inspector seemed to take great pleasure in producing his draconian warning:

- Shopkeepers MUST pay a fine for breach of health and safety standards.
- Produce sold on site putting the public at risk will be SOLELY the shop's responsibility.

It was a unique introduction to corner shop life. Take on a property that smelled as rancid as its gone-off dairy products and be told off for a major blunder on the part of the previous owners, who'd remained oblivious to their privileged position of feeding a nation.

Despite her petite 5 foot 2 inch frame and the fact that she was a shopkeeping novice, Mum did not take any shit. She took great pleasure in her retort:

- Why has the HSE neglected (for decades) to issue a fine to the previous owners?
- Was it not the case that THEY had failed to protect the great British public from rotten eggs and gone-off milk?

Sheepishly, the HSE man mumbled an excuse and hurriedly walked out of the door. We never saw him or the HSE again. The industrial-sized refrigerator arrived the next morning.

Despite its neglected state, the shop had retained a solid customer base and the previous owners were as easily forgotten as the dirty dishwater they'd left behind. Our family knew how to please, with a daily mantra of 'keep your door open, your mouth shut and smile sweetly at any passing trade'.

Mum soon got to know the lie of the land. But the promise of a 'perfect business solution' for a young mother of three was far from accurate. Help was needed. And every customer that walked through the door was a potential candidate. Little did they know that the

conversations over the counter about their family strug-
gles were an application for a job, and before long two
willing employees had joined the team. The daily grind of
stocking shelves and serving customers could now be
shared among three women who were all juggling their
own domestic lives. Within weeks, Mum had transformed
herself into boss.

The 1970s was a decade of change for women. Indira
Gandhi was leading a government in India and by the end
of the decade Margaret Thatcher became Britain's first
female prime minister. Within six years of arriving in
Britain, Mum had also climbed the ladder, from house-
wife to factory worker and now entrepreneur. She was in
charge and it felt good. Immigrant families who had
decided to become shopkeepers would often choose one
partner to go it alone while the other continued to make
money elsewhere, so Dad continued to work in the factory.
It was decided that the arrangement covered all bases
should anything go wrong, and of course two jobs meant
double the income.

Mum eased into shop life with a false sense of security that was perpetuated by unusually sociable work
hours, as this grocery shop didn't have the headache of
having to receive newspapers at 5 a.m. every morning.
With paid help, a working fridge, a solid clientele and
an 8.30 a.m. to 6 p.m. schedule, the shop plodded along
just fine.

But failed government policy brought the first real test.
Paraffin was about to keep the shopkeepers of Britain

extremely busy – and in profit. Plagued by years of industrial action, 1970s Britain was used to its dimly lit surroundings. Power cuts and shopping in the dark had become a fact of life. But in 1973 the Conservative prime minister Edward Heath declared that the country was in a state of emergency – the fourth time he had done so in his three short years as the country's leader. The war in the Middle East had pushed oil prices higher and supply to the West fell. At home, miners opted to work to rule, rejecting a pay cap and pushing coal reserves to critically low levels. The government acted, and its decision to restrict power supply forced the country into a three-day working week and pushed many families close to the breadline.

The use of electricity to heat shops and offices, operate street lights or advertising was banned. Anything reliant on a power supply was in trouble. The country had to adjust to wartime-like conditions (without the bombs) and get used to life by candlelight. It became the norm. Heath left office in 1974, failing to take the country's power problems with him. The electricity supply was still precarious and power could be cut off without warning. By the late 1970s, around 50 per cent of homes were experiencing regular power cuts[*].

For some, business was tough and the blackouts damaged their income. But for shopkeepers, who happened

---

[*] 'Decade that dimmed – the strike-hit Seventies', Robert Colville, *Daily Telegraph*, 29 July 2006

to be the main suppliers of paraffin in the area, business was far from gloomy. With many households reliant on paraffin, Mum had to learn the art of refilling canisters and servicing demand. Customers would queue for top-ups on an almost daily basis, and seeing their desperate faces was enough incentive to get to grips with the paraffin trade, and quickly.

It was not so much a difficult task as a time-consuming one, and Mum was overwhelmed by the daily rigmarole. Every week a large lorry would drop off a mammoth, 10-foot-by-10-foot metal paraffin tank, which was housed at the back of the property, away from the shop floor and kept under lock and key. This was a calculated move. Such was the universal desire for fuel that people attempting to get hold of it by illicit means was an ever-present risk.

Queues would snake around the shop wall, each customer clutching their oil carrier, eager for another top-up. It was quite a sight to behold. Containers varied from large buckets to metal vessels that, once topped up, would often require two pairs of hands to get home. The queues and multiple visits, although welcome financially, were becoming as burdensome as the gallons of paraffin itself.

Mum and Dad decided that the existing 'top up at any time' policy needed overhauling. It was time for a new edict. To ease the burden of all-day paraffin refills, from then on the customer would be obliged to obey the following rule:

Paraffin cans are to be dropped off in the morning only, and will be ready for collection between 4 and 6 p.m. Monday to Saturday.

It was a bold move for the new shopkeepers. But the 'take it or leave it' policy proved a big success. Some thirty or forty makeshift paraffin containers arrived the following morning and without complication or drama each was refilled and ready for collection later that day. Mum had once again played the role of captain superbly and the new regime went unchallenged. Any customer who was aggrieved by it remained silent. There were two paraffin suppliers in town; both of them corner shops situated half a mile apart. In much the same way as with ration books during and after the Second World War, the shop was too convenient an option to secure a much-needed product to risk waging war with the owner over how it was supplied. The only other alternative would be to line up at the paraffin trucks which were often situated in random locations across town.

Paraffin created an extra source of profit for a time, but the country was moving on and so were the Sharmas. Thatcher took on the mining unions, and deregulation of the energy industry put an end to the long-drawn-out blackouts of the 1970s. It was time to move on from the supply and demand of paraffin. It was time to let loose some ambition.

A shopkeeper with ambition is a powerful combination.

If you've ever made a 'unique purchase decision' in a corner shop you probably won't realise until after you've handed over your money how that power has worked. But when you bought those sickly sweet silver-ball cake toppings, which you'll never use but convinced yourself you would as you picked them from the vibrant display at the counter while paying it's because, my friend, you were reeled in by the entrepreneurial prowess of a corner shop owner. This is a small scale example, but all shopkeepers are always on the lookout for bigger and better opportunities.

But the shopkeeper isn't always the one in control – such are the demands of shop life that conversations between husband and wife about their financial concerns are generally conducted in the only time they have together: juggling stock checks, shelf-stacking and serving customers. So Mum and Dad were oblivious to the eavesdropping builder who had entered the shop the day they were locked in an animated discussion about buying another business. The builder took the liberty of sharing with them the news of a business that was for sale on the other side of town. The shop, he said, was a GOLD MINE. Under the spell of imagined profit, they hung on his every word, and thus a five-minute chat with a random builder over the purchase of a packet of cigarettes plotted the course of our family's next adventure. Mum turned up the radio, which was belting out Bucks Fizz's 'Making Your Mind Up', and the giant paraffin tank affectionately nicknamed 'Metal Mickey' looked on as my folks sashayed with excitement about what the future might hold.

It all seemed too good to be true. We were falling into a pit of success.

7

Captains of Industry

'Captain of industry': A business leader whose means of amassing a personal fortune contributed positively to the country in some way[*]

Margaret Thatcher was two years into her role as Prime Minister when Mum and Dad became owners of shop number two in 1981, positions that elevated all of them to new heights and brought reward and loss in equal measure.

In their twenty-two years as shopkeepers, Mum and Dad took on three shops. All brought challenges but none was as profitable as shop number two. We were moving into a world of selling newspapers and the goldmine territory of a newsagents. It also moved our family out of the 'go to' place for immigrants into a completely white landscape. The small suburb of Caversham, which residents

---

[*] 'Fine Line Between Thief and Entrepreneur', Philip Scranton, teaching history.org, 2011

will inform you 'is not Reading, darling, but Berkshire', is a quaint neighbourhood that straddles the River Thames and is best described as almost middle class.

According to the 1981 census for Caversham, my parents took the total of residents born in India and now living in the Berkshire suburb to thirty-three. At least ten of the other thirty were known to be associated with a corner shop, a shop in a parade of other shops, or a shop that was more like a mini-supermarket. Thus, in a white population of 9,398, my parents stood out. And it was here, as I peered over the counter on my tippy toes towards the world outside, that I began to understand what it really meant to be Asian shopkeepers in Britain.

Within weeks of opening our doors to the Caversham public, a neighbour decided to pop by and give Dad a piece of friendly advice:

Customer: I think it's good you don't open on Christmas Day, Mr Sharma.

Dad: Oh?

Customer: Yes. You see people round here don't like that, they see it as disrespectful. Him across the road, he opened on Christmas Day and I don't think he did much business. Yeah, do the right thing. You'll get a lot of respect for that one, you will.

Dad: [silence]

Customer: You into cricket then, Mr Sharma?

Dad: Oh yes, I love cricket.

Customer: Ah great, we're going to get on just fine then.

We knew what was needed to keep the customers happy. It wasn't rocket science, GCSE-level science or even make-it-up-as-you-go-along science. It was simple: a smiling face, bucket loads of diplomacy, and plenty of fags, booze and newspapers.

By the 1980s, 50 per cent of independent corner shops had been taken over by Asian families* and the traditional corner shop had evolved into something completely unrecognisable. By occupying that neglected space at the bottom of the street, the corner shop catapulted Asians like my mum and dad into the centre of British life. Punjabis and East African Asians all signed up to an unwritten pact: work as if your life depends on it. It was a work ethic that attracted much attention from the local community.

Cigarettes were the shop's big draw in those days and a display behind the counter enabled our customers to enjoy an unobstructed view of all the brands on offer. There were many, including Lambert & Butler, Embassy No. 1 and John Player Special. The shop was full of A2 cigarette advertisement posters, which all seemed to play up the glamour of smoking. It was an era some thirty years behind the law regulating

---

* 'Local Shop Report 2016', The Association of Convenience Stores

standardised packaging carrying graphic warnings of its dangers.

Cigarette manufacturers were very good at selling a mysterious and aspirational world where only the grown-ups were allowed in. An advert for a golden-coloured box of Benson and Hedges 100s carried the slogan:

'If you got crushed in your clinch with a soft pack, try our hard pack'.

The phrase is printed across the image of a young, beautiful blonde woman in a slinky dress pictured in a tight embrace with a tall, dark-haired man, her lips puckered just enough to make you feel as if you're getting a sneak peek into their private passion. The smoker-man slips us a suggestive glance from under a raised eyebrow, indicating that it's his lucky night. To a six-year-old kid living in a corner shop, however, it looked more like a man repelling bad breath and in desperate need of a wee.

Fortunately, I never had the guts or the height to get acquainted with the titty mags on the top shelf. That was a job reserved for my poor mum, a conservative woman by nature who had no vices beyond being an avid watcher of the American TV soaps *Dynasty*, *Dallas* and *The Colbys*.

There were three staple diets of TV consumption in the 1980s in our house. Dad's must-see (which inadvertently meant we all had to see it) was the nine o'clock news. Late as it was for us as children, it was the first chance after a long day in the shop for us to sit together as a family, eat dinner and not breathe the same air as the customers.

I would often divulge the inner workings of my home life with the parents of my friends from school. Going round for tea at their houses was exciting not only because of the decent home-cooked nosh but also for the chance to be in a house with a front door and a doorbell. It was a cheap source of entertainment, albeit an annoying one for my friends' parents, who would watch their daughter and her Asian friend running in and out of their home squealing with excitement as the entire family would receive yet another assault to their eardrums from my incessant ringing of the doorbell, which would chime for approximately five seconds each time it was pressed.

Doorbells and home-made chicken pie were the sources of much fascination to a corner shop kid like me, who welcomed the change from a Fray Bentos chicken and mushroom that we'd grab from the shop as a quick-fix supper. In the freedom of these places I'd let loose and quiz the family on why we were setting the dinner table at 5.30 p.m. It was only after my mouth had run away with details of my own family's late night dinnertime regime that an expression of concern would cloud their faces. Clearly our family life was not the norm.

A lifelong habit of not being punctual was probably established during these formative years. Our evenings ran so late I'd have a problem getting out of bed for school the next day, and most mornings could be spotted running to class while brushing my hair, with my satchel dangling off my left arm as if it too had been reluctantly dragged out of bed. But dinner in front of the nine o'clock news was worth staying up for.

On an almost daily basis, a bearded man with glasses would appear on a news report that would strangely alter the audio levels of our television set. At the age of ten and on closer examination, I deduced that this man had the power to adjust the volume controls and transform his voice into that of a strange alien whenever he appeared. This was the source of much curiosity, and I would intently watch to see if tonight would be the night that the strange voice would match the movements of the bearded man's lips. Nine and a half times out of ten it did not. The half being the moment that I was almost cheering in excitement for a perfect match, but it was always swiftly let down by an 'umm' that had been voiced over in the wrong place.

The bearded man turned out to be the Sinn Féin leader Gerry Adams, who at the time was subject to a broadcasting restriction by the British government that barred him and the members of eleven other organisations from speaking on radio or TV. Broadcasters quickly found a way to get around the ban by dubbing in – badly – an actor's voice.

Another evening must-see in our house was *Spitting Image*. It was Mum's favourite programme, and after Dad had had his fix of current affairs, once a week Mum would swap channels to get some much-needed light relief after a long day working in the shop. The satirical puppet show would mock the famous faces of the day and sketches featuring Margaret Thatcher and Ronald Reagan proved to be particularly popular in our household. The series would detail the so-called 'special relationship' between Britain and America in humorous fashion by suggesting a love interest between the two leaders: '*Well, so long, hunny-bun. What a fine-lookin' woman. Pity I'm only screwing her country!*'

Finally, we were all addicted to the goings-on at Southfork and the American soap opera *Dallas*, but you couldn't go five minutes without Mum switching channels when JR Ewing was involved in a compromising position with a love interest. The most uncomfortable moments weren't the ones spent watching people make love on the family's television screen, though – they were the times Mum miscalculated how long JR would be feeling amorous for and switched back mid-flow. Poor Mum. Any scenes of nudity and lovemaking were deemed inappropriate and she was adamant that her children would not be subjected to such filth; storylines of double-dealing, backstabbing and murder, however, were fine.

Unlike Maggie, who only had to worry about the apples and pears in their grocer's shop, we had embarked on a different kind of adventure – one that required longer hours, less sleep and more ink print on your hands. Owning a newsagent's was seen as a money generator. And soon we were acquainted with the concept of the passing trader – an unfamiliar face grabbing a newspaper or a pint of milk rather than spending an hour perusing the beautiful array of groceries. A newsagent's was all about quick sales at peak times of the day which meant that, as new owners, Mum and Dad had to say goodbye to the 8.30 a.m. to 6 p.m. of shop number one. In order to climb the ladder of corner shop success it was time to get serious. We were heading into the territory of what is known as an 'open all hours' culture. Although as new entrants into this foray we were designated *freshers*, softly cushioned by a 5.30 a.m. to 9.30 p.m. six day regime instead of the twenty-four hour, round-the-clock service that was gaining popularity among other Asian shopkeepers. This would have been a step too far for Mum and Dad, who were just about coming to terms with the early morning wake-up calls.

A little small for manual labour, I would help with the basic task of sitting on the bundles of newspapers waiting to be returned to the wholesaler at the end of the day. Dad's hands told the story of his endless encounters with the annoying blue plastic tape that bound these papers. The heavy-duty strip would take no prisoners so you'd need a Stanley knife to cut through it, but once slit apart the tape would snap back viciously in a Cobra-like attack and bite hard into the side of your hand, leaving a line much deeper and longer-lasting than a paper cut.

While Dad's hands bore the marks of the trade, his face told a story of the daily grind. Dad worked a pattern of six nights a month at Mars, and the night shift freed up time for him to help run the shop during the day. But it was a regime that kept him and our family on the edges of sanity. A 10 p.m. to 7 a.m. night shift would see Dad return to the shop in the morning and grab a bite to eat before catching a few hours of precious sleep. He'd then prise himself from bed around midday to head to the cash and carry and work his way through the stocklist of items that Mum had prepared earlier. Having returned to base and unloaded the goods, he'd replenish essential items on the shelves before minding shop to give Mum a much needed break. Luckily, Dad would manage to steal another nap before the shift cycle began again.

Paper cuts and lack of sleep are all part of the deal, because, regardless of whether we're seen as unsung heroes or unwelcome guests, corner shop success rests on following a simple business model: work your backside off. And don't just work your own backside off; make cousins, uncles and aunts work theirs off too. Anyone who was part of the 'family', biological or otherwise, could not escape a shift behind the shop counter or a bit of shelf-stacking. We all, at some point, had to take one for the team. Free family labour helped to reduce the amount in paid wages and added a few coppers to the family piggy bank.

The level of enjoyment afforded by shop work can probably best be divided along age parameters – enjoyment of it before adolescence and the pain of it afterwards. Under the age of ten, sweets were my domain. The plastic tubs of sherbet flying saucers and traffic lollipops were products I was particularly fond of. Ask me the price of any sweet we stocked and I almost always knew it. If I guessed incorrectly, I was allowed a margin of error of half a penny. It was a game my sisters and I enjoyed with varying success. Rows of penny sweets were positioned discriminatingly far from the sweet jars as if the latter occupied a special position in the social standing of confectionery.

'My' sweets were housed in lid-free plastic square containers. Smiley-faced pink mushroom designs would often cause confusion among kids who'd dive into a tub expecting chewy marshmallows and be greeted by choco-late bananas instead. Disclaimer: Correct restocking of tubs is at the shopkeeper's discretion.

I was pretty good at not tasting all the merchandise in one go, but admittedly I had a few weak moments. A particular favourite were the packets of fizzy crackle that would explode in your mouth as you tipped your head back and emptied the contents into your beak. It was the source of much entertainment, as I'd run to my sister's ear so she could hear the ridiculous goings-on in my mouth.

Of course, I wasn't the only one. Around 3.30 on most weekday afternoons you'd see the kids of Caversham leave our shop with their small white paper bags of good-ies. Some would devour gobstoppers that would turn their lips and tongue bright red. Others could be spotted chew-ing furiously on Toffos as their mouths contorted in all directions. Whatever your sweets of choice were, though, they were to be guarded with your life. Even though I occupied a safe spot as shopkeeper's daughter, I too was intensely territorial over my stock.

It is, however, a failing of humans in general and greedy children in particular to want what you can't have. Bored of my mini-empire, I decided to eye up the grand prize of the sweet kingdom – the glass jars. The sweet jars were positioned on the third shelf to the left of the shop's counter. Pristine jars with white plastic screw-top lids sat neatly on bright blue shelving. Here, some of the nation's favourite sweets could be found. The line-up from left to right was as follows:

When chosen by an excited child with a damp palm full of coins, some lucky sweets would find themselves joyously escaping from their glass confines to be weighed and pocketed in thin off-white paper bags. Our scales continued in the tradition of days gone by, when they were used to measure out bags of sugar or flour. Back then, it wasn't unheard of for shopkeepers to fiddle the scales and place an extra weight at the base of the bowl below a customer's eyeline. Such deception would add at least a few pence to a bag of sugar that you thought was being measured out honestly.

The scales in shop number two were too upstanding for such shenanigans, however. The shiny silver bowl stood proud atop a white Formica stand and to me it seemed the perfect place to stand and stretch out my arms to grab the jars, which had hitherto been out of bounds. The attempt to reach the brightly coloured lemon bon bons ended in a costly mistake: £273, to be precise. The scales broke with the weight of my six-year-old body, but heavier still was my heart as it sank to the bottom of the ocean as the consequences of what I'd done became apparent. Mum and Dad didn't have the time or extra pennies to cope with staff misdemeanours of this kind. If they'd had a choice I would've been served with a P45 on the spot, but a severe telling-off and a slap across my leg were enough to mark my memory.

Our shop tasks were minimal in comparison to the 4.30 a.m. wake-up call Mum would get when the newspapers were delivered an hour before opening time.

Newspapers had replaced paraffin as the big profit-maker, but with them came the promise of a broken night's sleep.

Dozen of crates of red-top and blue-top milk bottles would quickly follow the bundles of newspapers, rattling in their large green crates that were usually damp from the morning dew. Dad would roll in bleary-eyed from an overnight shift at Mars as Mum and the delivery men lamented the ungodly hour of doing business. The only other person stirring at that time of the morning was Mrs Bradley, who was waiting for our doors to open so she could try (yet again) to get her hands on a bottle of much-needed vodka. The daily scenario would follow a pattern of chat–attempt–refusal. Mum would courteously refuse Mrs Bradley's whining overtures to serve her alcohol outside of the licensed hours of 11 a.m. to 11 p.m. If ever Mum had a weak moment (which she never did) it would have cost the shop its alcohol licence. Nothing was worth that, even if Mrs Bradley was promising cash payment at double – or at times triple, depending on her desperation levels – the price of her beloved 1 litre of Smirnoff vodka. Life in shop number two was hard. If Dad wasn't working in the factory, he was doing a cash-and-carry run for the shop. If Mum wasn't on the shop floor serving the customers and stacking the shelves, she was in the kitchen cooking for us. Junior help was more about childcare than it was about free family labour.

My pin-ups at the time were Andrew Ridgeley and George Michael, whose pictures I snaffled from our stocks of *Just*

Seventeen and *Smash Hits*. (It was a perk of the job to peruse the magazines for free to pass the time when trade was slow.) Maggie, however, was more concerned with courting a different kind of poster boy, and by the early 1980s the Asian shopkeeper was a figure at the heart of the community and was championed by the prime minister.

Early 1980s Britain was in the grip of a brutal recession. The country was buckling under the strain of mass unemployment and growing social divisions. The jobless total topped three million in 1983 and inflation was at record levels. Maggie and her boys in government needed something to show the country that all was okay. The prime minister searched out a success story to proclaim her economic policy was working, and thus it was decided that this daughter of a grocer would champion the Asian shopkeeper.

To be fair, it wasn't the first time politicians had played the race card in this way. Each political party of the 1970s and 1980s had a go at adopting the powerful image of the Asian entrepreneur as their own. But none did it better than the Conservatives, who went so far as to take out full-page newspaper ads in the late 1970s:

> *Is setting you apart from the rest of society a sensible way to overcome racial prejudices and social inequality? The question is, should we divide the British people instead of uniting them? To the Labour Party you are a Black Person. To the*

Conservative Party you are a British Citizen. Vote Conservative and you vote for a more equal, prosperous Britain.[*]

The Tories loved us. The Asian man embodied the Conservative values of hard work and aspiration. Here was a convenient way for the government to suggest that Britain was a meritocratic society, as personified by Asian shopkeepers across the land. It was a bold PR move designed to encourage native Britons to take their cue from the many ethnic faces that were now part of everyday British life. 'Look how well they're doing – you too can do as well as them.' The ramifications of such objectification were ignored. The consequences of politically 'pimping out' the Asian shopkeeper would last longer than it took for a Tory PR man to guzzle a wee whisky in Westminster's Smoking Room.

The Tories were on shaky ground, however – just two decades earlier they hadn't been quite so fond of their immigrant friends:

Face the facts. If you desire a coloured for your neighbour, vote Labour. If you're already burdened with one, vote Tory.[†]

[*] Conservative Political Party Advert, 1978 (created by Saatchi & Saatchi)
[†] Conservative Political Party flyer from Lambeth, 1964

This advert from 1964 claimed that once in office, the Conservative Party would expel these immigrants, and this proclamation was made a good few years before Enoch Powell's epiphany. Oddly enough, it was published just as a twenty-four-year-old Indian man was filling out an employment voucher application in his backyard in Delhi.

The Labour Party had simultaneously had a go at immigrants and was responsible for further reducing the rights of Commonwealth citizens. The Commonwealth Immigrants Act of 1968 discriminated against Commonwealth citizens in an effort to try to restrict the flow of immigration to the UK. It was later challenged for being in breach of Britain's constitutional responsibility under colonial governance rules.

It was unlikely that the politicians cared much about exploiting people like my parents as the apparent models of economic success. And in return what was going on in the halls of Westminster had little practical impact on the corner shop trade. Asian businesses were doing very well and by the 1980s you were seven times more likely to be a millionaire if your surname was Patel rather than Smith.* Mum and Dad were neither Patels nor millionaires but the sheer man-hours they put in were paying off. Nevertheless, being used as political fodder left a bitter taste. It also left a bitter taste in the mouths of people who were not enjoying this apparent good

* 'The Rich List' Dr Philip Beresford, *The Sunday Times* (2000)

fortune, and putting Asian shopkeepers on some kind of political pedestal meant that we could be toppled at any time – and there were plenty who wanted the chance to knock us off the perch. An opportunity for doing just that was looming.

The immigration of thousands of Commonwealth workers into Britain had created a melting pot of cultures and with it a whole array of issues. 'Strange' people with different languages, dress and culture were now openly rubbing shoulders with the white working class of Britain's cities on some of the poorest streets. In the 1980s, in the dark days of unemployment and recession, visible differences between the natives and the non-natives were seized upon and utilised in the darkest of times. The far right movement was gaining ground and a diverse nation was being prized apart along racial lines.

For some reason, and despite Britain's love for it, curry became synonymous with the identity of a whole people. We didn't actually smell of curry but apparently, for some, it was okay to suggest we did. I can see why you might say that a fishmonger or a fish and chip shop owner smelled of fish. But we were not restaurateurs, we were shopkeepers, and there'd be no chance of grabbing a curry while buying your newspaper – my folks were already working round the clock as it was. (Having said that, I have been to a corner shop that serves food and marvelled at the success of their business model. There's nothing quite like chomping on steaming, freshly made samosas as you do your weekly shop!) The Irish, as far as I can tell – and I am married to one – do not smell of potatoes. Chinese people have not been accused of smelling of wonton soup, so why was it deemed appropriate to suggest that all Indians smell of curry?

Some customers were more vocal than others. To walk into a corner shop and proclaim 'it stinks in here' felt like a punch in the face. Perhaps the speaker was unaware of the shit on the sole of their shoe that they'd walked in with them. This was 1980s Britain, after all, before the arrival of 'poop a scoop', when stepping in dog muck was a regular occurrence. Fortunately our family largely escaped such insults but others told us how quickly the customer banter could turn nasty.

It's beside the point, but we didn't eat as much curry as I would have liked anyway. Time constraints of having two full-time working parents meant that frozen food or microwave meals were appreciated during particularly busy times in the shop. If one believes the saying that you are what you eat, then technically we were a half-Indian, half-Findus family. At least three times a week we would consume a Findus product of some kind, as did a generation of children who were born and brought up in the 1970s and 1980s. Their French-bread pizzas and crispy pancakes were staple foods in our house, alongside Fray Bentos pies and boil-in-the-bag cod with a parsley sauce. All, of course, were readily available from our shop.

When preparing these foods, however, what you aren't supposed to do is set fire to them while your parents are busy minding shop and entrusting their darlings to help them out by cracking on with making tea. Shop life requires corner shop kids to grow up quickly, but the added responsibility of acting grown-up comes with its own problems. On one occasion my eldest sister got a little too enthusiastic with the oil-pouring into the frying pan, and within seconds our much-loved chicken and bacon crispy pancakes were up in flames. The pancakes would usually burn the inside of your mouth, not your kitchen, and the incident happened during a particularly busy time in the shop due to a late-afternoon surge in customer activity.

As the flames grew and our dinner burned, it was a customer who heard the screams emanating from the back of the shop. 'Mrs Sharma, I think I can hear your daughter screaming . . .' Mum apologised for having to leave the shop floor in a hurry to see what all the fuss was about. It took her no longer than Usain Bolt running the 100 metres to calm the pandemonium. In Wonder Woman fashion, she grabbed the frying pan with the charred remains of our dinner, chucked it into the garden and got back to the shop floor to resume service. 'That'll be 99p, please.' Disaster averted, we had baked beans on toast that night.

Another family favourite consisted of French-bread pizza accompanied by ice cream served with Ice Magic – a chocolate sauce that hardens to a crunchy shell as soon as you pour it onto ice cream. This was corner shop nutrition at its best, and we all had a constitution that was built in the 1980s. Every product we sold was tried and tested at home. Should a customer ever need advice on what to try, one of the Sharma girls could oblige with a mark out of ten.

Occasionally we'd be asked fashion advice too. Ladies en route to a night out would stop by to pick up a bottle of bubbles and ask us what we thought of their attire. With crimped hair and a large silk polka dot bow hair clip I wasn't much of a fashionista, but clearly that didn't matter when an opinion was demanded in a hurry. Of course, the variety of looks would always be given a thumbs up by us, even though I was somewhat perplexed by the fingerless-lace-gloves in the middle of winter or the excessive use of blue eye-shadow that went well above the brow bone into the eyebrow itself.

My mum's corner shop uniform was an entirely Western outfit of trousers and a jumper. The only Indian feature, aside from her skin colour, was the red dot on her forehead. Mum has worn a bindi since she got married, and for Hindu women it's a tradition that dates back centuries. Traditionally the bindi is placed between the eyebrows and is said to be the sixth chakra and the seat of concealed wisdom. Mum channelled a lot of wisdom during her years as a shopkeeper, especially when the bindi became the topic of fascinated conversation:

Customer: 'Do you pencil it on, Mrs Sharma, or is it a stick-on? Does it come off? Do you sleep with it on?'

Who'd have thought that years later the red dot would become a must-have fashion accessory, with Madonna and Beyoncé popularising this sacred Hindu tradition. The truth is, at that point we were some way off that level of acceptance.

A long way off.

8

The P Shop

'Paki', noun (BRITISH *informal offensive*): *A person from Pakistan or South Asia by birth or descent, especially one living in Britain*

To be a corner shop owner is a choice. And choices seem like the right ones when they have good outcomes. A good day might go something like this:

- DELIVERIES: On time.
- SLEEP: Five hours! Whoopee!
- CUSTOMERS: All our regulars. We love them.
- MONEY MADE: A LOT.
- RACIST INCIDENTS: None.
- Additional Comments: I love my job and all that it brings me. Thank you, Universe, for my life.

A bad day, on the other hand, might look like this:

- DELIVERIES: Milkman late. Newspapers a 'no show'.

- SLEEP: Two and a half hours. Disturbed by bedwetting child.
- CUSTOMERS: Moody. Complaint – paper boy delivered damp newspaper (it was pissing down with rain).
- MONEY MADE: Average. Suspected theft of 2 Double Decker bars and a Marathon.
- RACIST INCIDENTS: Just one. Teenager shouted 'Paki' after request to buy cigarettes was refused.
- Additional Comments: Must stock Clearasil for spotty teens.

The racist term 'Paki' acquired its offensive connotations in the 1960s when it was used to refer to anyone who looked Asian (another foul word was used for Afro-Caribbeans). This meant that Indians, Bangladeshis, Iraqis, Iranians and Pakistanis were all in the line of fire. The first instances of 'Paki bashing' were recorded in the 1960s and were ruthless, violent acts carried out by white, usually male, youths who would target anyone who looked Asian. Aside from anything else, 'Paki' is a hugely inaccurate term. Our family is originally from India so we are not Pakistani at all. Although Dad was born in the part of India that is now Pakistan, thanks to Partition, I'm not entirely sure that qualifies him for inclusion either. But even if we *were* all from Pakistan, the term remains hugely offensive.

To perpetrate an act of hate can be a complicated affair. It requires forward planning and the ability to execute a task that ensures your victim be rendered helpless in the face of evil. In the 1970s, for the Asian immigrant, that evil was often conveyed with the aid of a milk bottle – or ten, to be precise.

Ten empty milk bottles tied to a piece of heavy-duty string can be a cheap and easy way to inflict racial harassment. The 'string of empty milk bottles on the door handle' trick was much used in the Reading area to persecute black and Asian households, including that of my parents, who at the time were a young couple settling into a new home and about to welcome their first child into the world. The perpetrator would tie the milk bottles to the door handle of the victim, and when the victim opened their door in the morning it would cause the entire group of bottles to come crashing down and smash all over the ground.

There wasn't much point in reporting these incidents to the police, as Dad soon found out – when he headed to the police station after yet another one of these episodes, he was told in no uncertain times that there was little the police could do to help. Dad, he was told, was the fifth person that weekend to have filed such a complaint. His plea for assistance was redundant, because the police were too overwhelmed with filling out report cards and paperwork to catch the perpetrators of this banal activity. It was common knowledge that those responsible for these attacks were bored teenagers, who would later become affiliated to the National Front, which occupied a base just a mile away from our family's doorstep.

Milk bottles at least didn't endanger your person. But one evening in 1974, as he sipped a pint of lager in the pub, Dad came very close to being the victim of a much more serious attack. Thanks to a friendly pub landlord who had a watchful eye on my father, it was an event he managed to escape.

Dad had struck up a friendship with the owner of his local pub, with whom he would enjoy a necessary pint and a chat on his way home from a shift on the factory floor. Both men enjoyed football, and in 1974 England had failed to qualify for the World Cup, so they had plenty to chat about. Dad, being a Chelsea supporter, would recount tales of his unsuccessful attempts to scale the walls of Stamford Bridge, while the publican took great pleasure in predicting their downfall. He was right. Chelsea, Luton Town and Carlisle United were relegated at the end of the season.

The evening in question began unremarkably. Dad was on the day shift, which enabled him to feel vaguely human since he could clock in and out at a sociable hour and, like most of his neighbours, stop by the pub to enjoy a cool pint of John Smith's before his short five-minute walk home. While he did so, the friendly pub landlord became aware of a group of rather unsavoury characters who had taken a particular interest in Dad and were watching him as he sat on his usual stool across from the bar, enjoying his drink. All of a sudden, Dad was politely told to 'do one' by his friend, who had overheard the five white men discussing how they could target Dad once they had finished their round of beers.

The men drank their pints at a leisurely pace, which afforded Dad enough time to make a quick exit. Who knew that 'Paki bashing' was such a thirsty activity? Dad managed to escape unhurt but he was alarmed at the thought that he'd nearly been beaten up solely on the basis of his skin colour. The landlord told him to lie low for a few days and his beloved ritual of stopping off for a pint was brought to an abrupt halt by a group of men who were out hunting like a pack of wolves. Thankfully this close encounter was never repeated, and after a week or so Dad plucked up the courage to walk back into the pub and resume his chat with the landlord about how Chelsea had beaten Arsenal in the London Derby earlier in the week.

Many of the perpetrators of these savage attacks were skinheads sympathetic to far right groups such as the National Front (later the British National Party), and plenty of them came by our shop in the early 1980s. To a primary-age child they were an intriguing species, and I used to watch them from the perfect spot: a glass-fronted fridge window that provided a reflection of the entire shop floor. Through the rows of Yoplait dessert pots and Fruit Corners, I could spy on every customer. I was Uatu of the Fantastic Four, watching over our kingdom for any sign of danger.

It being the 1980s, though, the hard part was telling the racist skinheads from the punks. Both shaved their heads so close to the scalp that you could see the nip marks from the razor blade; both wore black leather jackets and Doc Martens, and I found it troublesome to decipher one from the other. And it was an important distinction to make: a skinhead might potentially unleash a tirade of verbal abuse upon us, while a punk just had dodgy taste in music.

Britain was experiencing its worst recession since the Second World War and the idea that the immigrant worker who 'came to work for us' was now making money at a time of national crisis was the perfect way to stoke racial tensions. But there was also grave resentment towards the police from black and Asian youths who saw them as representatives of a white authoritarian 'racist' state. In 1981 a 'summer of discontent' saw Britain witness a series of violent riots, mostly in deprived inner-city areas.

The most famous were the Brixton riots in south London, which sparked 'copycat' riots across the country. The riots pitted black and Asian youths against the police, and scenes of violence with reports of fatalities dominated the headlines across mainstream media. Mum and Dad can still recall how for years the newspapers in the shop would carry at least one headline a day referencing Britain's racial tensions.

In true corner shop tradition, the shockwaves were discussed over the shop counter. Mum and Dad would ride out the conversations with a tactic of 'listening only'. The method worked well as they realised that keeping their opinions to themselves was the only way to survive the current mood of distrust.

Two days after the chaos and violence of Brixton, the UK government commissioned the Scarman Report, which warned of racial disadvantage and inner-city decline and called for a better, co-ordinated way of dealing with these problems.

At the time, many people within our extended family believed that the riots were largely about tension between black male youths and the police. But the deeper-seated reasons for the riots concerned all racial groups. Racial tensions that had bubbled to the surface in deprived urban areas attracted any ethnic group of colour. All became embroiled in one way or another during Britain's dark years of hate. It culminated in 1985 with the death of PC Keith Blakelock, a name that I remember well thanks to the media's endless coverage of the Broadwater Farm riot in Tottenham, north London. Blakelock's death received national coverage on TV, on the radio and in print – vastly more than the death of Cynthia Jarrett, an African-Caribbean woman, which had triggered the disturbances two days earlier that ultimately led to Blakelock's demise.

Chants of 'Enoch was right' could be heard in the mid 1980s; the country was divided, and far right groups were happy to capitalise on people's discontent. As Thatcher was insisting on how good the Asian shopkeeper was for Britain, the rest of the country seemed less convinced, and racial attacks on Asians and other minorities tripled. After numerous race riots and years of racial profiling, many victims felt isolated and alone. They had little faith in the police, and felt they simply had to put up and shut up.

Once held up as Tory success symbols, now Commonwealth workers and the multicultural faces of Britain were giving the government cause for concern due to the violence that had erupted. The race riots of the 1980s also came at the height of the troubles in Northern Ireland, and recent declassified documents reveal what Maggie was really thinking about them and us. In a peace-building summit in November 1984 with her Irish counterpart, Garret FitzGerald, Maggie voiced her concerns about the possibility of an Asian uprising if Irish nationalists were allowed to express their identity in Northern Ireland.

> Mrs Thatcher fretted about the wider consequences of addressing Catholic alienation in relation to ethnic minorities in Britain. She failed to understand why nationalists were calling for reforms in policing, justice, equality and power-sharing.
>
> She said: 'If these things were done, the next question would be what comes next? Were the Sikhs in Southall to be allowed to fly their own flag?'*

I was first introduced to Southall at around two weeks old. I don't remember it, of course, but our fortnightly visits to the area became part of my childhood and to this day it remains the best place to gorge on incredible Indian food, the likes of which you will not find in the thousands of bog-standard curry houses across the country. There is no Chicken

* Press Association, published in the *Daily Telegraph*, 27 December 2014

Vindaloo on the streets of Southall but rather good honest Punjabi food – the best in the country. (I'm still only about halfway through my nationwide quest for the best curry house, but Southall currently retains the number one spot.)

The west London suburb is the place to go for second-generation Asians who treat their parents on any given Father's or Mother's Day to a feast so big you'll need a lie-down afterwards. The real test of endurance, though, is when you have to navigate the hundreds of Southall's shops because you have a wedding in the family. No big fat Indian wedding prep is complete without the painstaking hours and days of bartering over bridal clothes, shoes and jewellery. It is in our DNA to haggle, and the results of some successful bargain-hunting can be seen in most Asian-run corner shops. Look closely and you might spot the multi-pack crisps from Asda that are being sold individually by your shopkeeper. It's what we call being a shrewd business operator, and what you might call being a cheeky bastard.

Southall was a regular location for a family meal out, particularly for a special occasion. We went there every year on my birthday – St George's Day – to do something appropriately patriotic: go for a curry. My birth date happens to have multiple links to Britain's history with immigration:

- 23 April 1968: 1,000 London dockers march in support of Enoch Powell's Rivers of Blood speech.
- 23 April 1977: British Asian baby born in Reading, Berkshire

- 23 April 1977: 3,000 anti-fascists battle with 1,000 National Front supporters on Duckett's Common, Wood Green
- 23 April 1979: Anti-fascist teacher Blair Peach killed in Southall race protests

This latter incident occurred when violence erupted during a protest against the National Front following the death of a Sikh teenager in a racist attack the previous year. It hardened a community to fight for justice, and clashes between the two sides proved fatal. Blair Peach, a teacher and anti-racist activist, was knocked unconscious during the demonstrations and later died.

It's hard to imagine that a place where I'd spent hours with my parents watching them scrutinise potatoes for flaws or check the firmness of a bitter gourd on the colourful fruit and veg stalls had been the scene of such violence and a senseless death.

But racial tensions were running high, and corner shops, now predominately run by the Asian community, were on the frontline. They were seen as soft, easy targets. The glass-fronted fridge may once have afforded me a sense of protection from danger but it was no protection for the shop as a whole, whose very position made it visible and vulnerable on the corners of Britain's streets. Areas that were home to high numbers of Asians saw the worst of the vandalism, with windows being smashed and excrement being pushed through letterboxes.

Once praised for being the hub of the community, the corner shop was now a prime target for attack. Verbal abuse would often escalate to violent confrontation as the far right movement gained an ever-wider public profile and ever greater support.

Somehow, we were the lucky ones. In the twenty-two years that my parents worked as shopkeepers, never once did anyone call them 'Paki'. No windows were smashed in shops number one, two or three and no shit was put through our letterbox. Yet years later, after they had pulled out of the corner shop trade, the term reared its ugly head in the most banal fashion.

Walking past my family's home, some random man spotted my mum and uncle in the driveway and in a high-pitched, almost friendly tone shouted 'Hello Paki'. It caught both of them by complete surprise and my mum had to restrain her brother from going after the idiot. It was *the* topic over dinner that night and there was a lot of laughter as Mum recalled how the random man had ruined an intense conversation she'd been having with my uncle about whether or not white spirit could shift the muck from the previously pristine white B&Q garden set that had got heavily weathered during the winter. Thankfully the muck didn't stick and one lick of the lethal liquid restored the furniture to its original glory, but later, while taking tea on the lawn (as one does in retirement), the memory of that idiotic man cast a shadow over an otherwise pleasant English summer's day.

I was always aware of the term, not because someone was vicious enough to say it to me, but because it had somehow found its way into everyday conversation in 1980s Britain, used without much thought or concern. The general public were so heedless of its racist connotations that it even regularly found its way onto primetime television, further 'legitimising' its use – particularly on the BBC. Here was a public service broadcaster, whose licence fee was being funded by Asian and black Britons, apparently deeming it acceptable to use racist terms for comedic value.

Shows such as *Till Death Do Us Part*, *Only Fools and Horses*, *Open All Hours* and *Mind Your Language* all attracted millions of people during peak-time viewing on a Saturday night or weekday evening. These sitcoms all followed the same format – canned laughter dubbed into scenes of apparently funny dialogue to make us, the viewers, laugh along too. Racist slurs didn't escape this post-production dub.

If the producers had listened to real-time reactions, there'd have been no need to edit in the laughter in our household. My parents joined in with the chorus of amusement. Millions would tune into such shows to see what Britain was up to. United by common experience, people felt that what they watched on their televisions was a reflection of what was going on on the doorsteps of the nation. It was better to laugh than to cry.

Perhaps the one character that best defined the impact of immigration on Britain was *Till Death Do Us Part*'s Alf Garnett, brilliantly played by the actor Warren Mitchell.

A white working-class man, 'Alf' had already spent two decades telling us what was wrong with British society. He was a devout Conservative supporter, but not a fan of Thatcher, who he firmly believed should be in the kitchen and not the cabinet. Alf Garnett was an anti-feminist, pro-monarchy, West Ham United-supporting, racist bigot. No doubt if he engaged in cultural norms today he'd enjoy millions of social media followers. Rarely did an episode of *TDDUP* go by without some reference to 'Pakis', 'coons' and 'Yids'. Alf Garnett regularly championed Enoch Powell, who in turn was referred to as a Garnett-like figure by critics seizing upon the character traits of a bigoted racist (albeit a middle-class one).

Just like Alf, other characters and shows of 1970s and 1980s Britain held up a mirror to the stark reality of multicultural Britain. So when in 2004 the BBC decided to run repeats of the beloved comedy *Only Fools and Horses*, they decided to edit out any 'offensive' language, including the term 'Paki'. There is a lot to edit.

Grandad: What's the point, all the animals will be dead, we won't be able to grow nothin' because all the earth will be contaminated. Where we gonna get something to eat?

Del Boy: Bound to be a little Paki shop open some-where. *

* 'The Russians Are Coming', *Only Fools and Horses*, Series 1, Ep. 6, 13 October 1981

139

But deleting the memories of what life was actually like at that time for Asians is not quite as simple as a cutting-room edit. The Alf Garnetts of this world have their place in history but for some bizarre reason, even though with hindsight the character is recognised as a vile racist, he – and other characters like him from TV's 'golden era' – is also the subject of great nostalgic affection.

The media was not responsible for inventing the term 'Paki', of course, but its liberal use during primetime family viewing made it socially acceptable. It also stuck in your head. It was much like the annoying, rather catchy theme tune that accompanied an advert selling R. Whites Lemonade from 1973 to 1984. The 'Secret Lemonade drinker' advertising campaign was a success and even won an award. It seemed to be on the telly as much as Mr Garnett. Forty years on, I am unable to erase Elvis Costello's unique rendition of 'Secret Lemonade Drinker'. It is lodged in the psyches of a generation who grew up at that time.

The word 'Paki' found its way into my world in more casual and insidious ways than just through TV, though. While other kids would hang out outside the shop looking cool, I was not able to enjoy such liberties. There is no way you can look cool hanging outside your own front door. My friend and I began experimenting with cigarettes, but such is the life of a corner shop kid that any attempt to be rebellious comes with pitfalls. My friend would encourage me to steal fags from our shop and bring them to school, instead of embarrassing herself by attempting to buy them from my mum – who would then in turn tell her mum. But in the same way that her dance teacher mother refused to give me free ballet lessons, I refused to provide free produce from our 'gold mine'. Perhaps I wasn't the friend she'd bargained for; the friend who had access to the Aladdin's Cave of penny sweets and cigarettes.

Fearing I'd be caught by Mum and Dad (which would result in the instant loss of a limb), I denied her request. And that was when life changed forever. Without batting an eyelid, she said casually: 'No problem, I'll just go to the Paki shop next door.'

In the same way that Newton was struck by a falling apple, I was hit by the off-hand way the 'P word' had entered my world in the course of a conversation with someone I actually liked. How was this possible? My brain suddenly malfunctioned, overloaded with confusion that my best friend had used *that* word. The context in which she'd innocently used it summed up a place, a people and an activity all in one go. She had revealed what she thought of my very being – me, my home, my family, their livelihood – in one heavily loaded word.

Immediately afterwards, she had already moved onto a new point of interest: whether I could get hold of *Just Seventeen* so that we could cut out more pictures of Morten Harket for our sticker book. It was then that I had my Eureka moment: the use of an offensive term does not in itself reveal a person's fundamental beliefs and intentions, especially when they are pubescent teens mimicking something they have seen or heard without fully understanding its meaning. I decided that her comment was therefore excusable, but anyone older would not be afforded such a liberty.

Years later, when I asked my friend about that moment, she too recalled it in vivid detail. She said she'd been surprised at how it had just come out of her mouth with no understanding of what impact it might have. Interestingly, she also remembers me nervously laughing with her as we walked on, minus cigarettes and without any mention of what had just been said. During this honest conversation she also admitted she wanted to ask me something that had been bugging her for almost a decade: 'Why did I never get to eat your mum's wonderful Indian cooking when I came round to yours for tea?'

I told her I couldn't imagine – maybe we just didn't have the right ingredients in at the time? But I knew damn well why she never got some of the best food I have ever eaten in my life. When friends came over, Mum was under strict instructions to only plate up McCain oven chips and Birds Eye fish fingers. I'd breathe a sigh of relief every time she played along with it. I doubt she knew I was embarrassed that my white friend might think us weird for having different foods and far worse, if she hated it, might never want to be my friend again.

Note to childhood self: *Must try harder to embrace own culture*.

Note to adult self: *Lying is bad, remember?*

The phrase 'Paki shop' was an inevitable extension of the P word, given that in 1980s Britain most Asians were in some way associated with the running of a local shop. But it doesn't require a high IQ to figure out how un-Pakistani most corner shops are, so for the people who insist on still using the term:

- The majority of corner shopkeepers in Britain come from India or East Africa, not Pakistan
- There was no produce in our corner shop, or in pretty much any corner shop past or present, that was made in or imported from Pakistan
- The only official 'Pakis' in the world is Te Arikinul Tuheitia Pakis, the seventh Maori monarch – King Pakis to you and me – who was crowned on 21 August 2006

Apparently those using the term weren't overly concerned with accuracy, however. Daubing the word 'Paki' across a corner shop wall or window was a common sight across inner cities in the 1980s. It's only surprising that Asian shopkeepers, who are never usually ones to miss an opportunity for self-promotion, did not use it to their advantage instead of wasting man-hours scrubbing the letters off their walls.

P – Please visit your
A – Asian shopkeeper for
K – Knockout prices
I – Inside a friendly shop

Having a corner shop was the dream for many migrants in the 1960s and 1970s. But by the 1980s, against a backdrop of racial tension, the dream was beginning to turn sour. I was aware of this in the daily grind of shop life but I hadn't seen the same issues mirrored in fiction until a random night of channel-hopping.

Way past my bedtime I was to stumble upon a film that changed my life. I can't exaggerate the impact this movie had on me as a child when I really shouldn't have been watching TV after the watershed at all. If it hadn't been for Mum and Dad being sidetracked by a stock take in the shop, I would not have got to watch *My Beautiful Laundrette*, which was broadcast on Channel 4 in 1985. The 18-rated movie contained acts of homosexuality, but more importantly scenes and dialogue that would scare the shit out of me:

Moose: Why you working for these people? Pakis?
Jonny: It's work, that's why! I wanna do some work for a change instead of all this hanging around. What, you jealous?
Moose: No. I'm angry, Jonny. I don't like to see one of ours grovelling to Pakis. Look, they came here to work for us. That's why we brought them over, okay? ... Look, don't cut yourself off from your own people.*

* Excerpt courtesy of Hanif Kureishi and Film4

The story of a British Pakistani boy who opens up a laundrette with his white punk boyfriend contains politics, race, violence and bigotry, and reveals just what life was like in 1980s Britain. It is also responsible for making a lasting impact on a British Asian child who was glued to the screen for the entire hour and thirty-five minutes' duration, before crawling into bed with a lasting impression of a world that existed outside the confines of our corner shop.

Just like in the film, in reality the sight of an Asian business doing well at a time of national crisis was a kick in the teeth. And we were doing well. By the mid-1980s our little corner shop was thriving, and every ping of the cash register was another pound note in the bank of Mum and Dad.

'Oh Mrs Sharma, you're so busy I queued for ten minutes for the paper this morning. You should get more staff in!' An innocent statement by one of our customers who just wanted a speedier service – but if you couldn't grab a pint of milk or a newspaper in under a minute you knew something was going on.

In Britain there has historically been nothing worse than seeing someone of colour doing well financially when white parts of the country are pissed off and out of work. Working-class resentment at this time was channelled along ethnic lines and the corner shop had little protection from potential threat. By the very nature of trading times, the shop would be open and closed during unsociable hours when fewer people were in sight for back up should a problem arise. The long hours and exhausting regime were paying off – but we weren't the only ones who knew about it.

It was 12.55 p.m. one Thursday afternoon in 1988 when Mum was shutting up the shop for an hour's lunch break. Mum loved these precious sixty minutes, and within half an hour of closing the shop at lunchtime she'd have eaten her lunch and grabbed a twenty-minute nap before reopening the shop at 2 p.m. The local customer base knew the shop's siesta time and on this particular occasion our neighbour Simon was the only other person around the shop, doing a few odd jobs in the garage at the back.

Five minutes before closing, a man walked into the shop and tried to buy a Mars bar with a twenty-pound note. Mum refused to serve him, partly on the basis that she didn't have any change in the till, and he was keeping her from a well-earned break. The man then returned, just a minute or so later, with a pound note in one hand and a Mars bar in the other. Mum accepted the purchase with her focus very much on serving the customer so she could get some rest. But as she opened the till to pass the man his change, he pulled a knife on her and, pushing her back, hurriedly started to clear the till for all the cash that was inside. The whole incident took only a couple of minutes. Simon, who heard Mum shouting, gave chase and grabbed the nearest thing he could get his hands on – an empty milk crate – and lobbed it at the robber. But the Mars bar man had made good on the seconds' advantage he'd had on Simon as he darted out of the shop.

The man got away with all that morning's takings, including all the money from the Football Pools coupons that were due to be collected later that day. Fortunately, what he hadn't seen was the bag of cash by Mum's feet on the right of the counter, ready for Dad to collect and drop off at the bank when he got home. Had the thief been more accomplished, he could have got away with more than a thousand pounds in that one bag alone. Instead he stole a hundred-odd pounds and years of confidence from a shopkeeper who had dedicated her life to serving the public.

The police came by the shop later that day to interview Mum, along with an artist who attempted to do a facial composite. Mum was suffering from shock and was thus unable to put forward an adequate description of the assailant for the drawing. Dad had to take a week off work following the incident as Mum was suffering from what we later found out was post-traumatic stress. At the time we thought that a lie-down and a week's rest would sort out her PTSD.

Dreams do not concern themselves with the passage of time and even now, at the age of seventy-four, Mum still suffers from a recurring dream of that incident back in 1988. The dream takes her back to the shop floor at 12.55 p.m., and the man walking in attempting to pay for a Mars bar with a twenty-pound note. The dream scenario, however, plays out somewhat differently as Mum becomes preoccupied with the exact positioning of the robber's knife. Her dream is full of activity and snapshots of moments replay in her mind as she desperately tries to work out where on earth the knife is. Both the man's hands are accounted for, one rapidly clearing the till and the other pushing against Mum's right shoulder. But there is no knife to be seen.

It's October 2017 and Mum shrugs her shoulders as she awakens with the realisation that another night's sleep has been disturbed by the thieving foe. Such is the legacy of corner shop life that some things don't fade away easily. I hope that one day knifegate will be replaced by a happier dream where Mum peruses the shelves as she walks about her kingdom and fondly welcomes a stranger through our shop door without fear or regret.

9

The Turf Wars

'Turf war', noun: A fight or an argument to decide who controls an area or an activity

A newspaper and a chocolate bar is a common pairing that we wouldn't give a second thought to as we ring them through the till. A pint of milk and a porn magazine, on the other hand, is not only going to attract attention, it will also encourage customer and shopkeeper to lock eyes for longer than is deemed comfortable.

My sister recalls entering a silent world that reached stratospheric levels of discomfort when she once served a sixteen-year-old trying to buy a porn mag. Such an event was not uncommon: a young lad would be sent out by his mother to buy a pint of milk, and decide to make the banal task more interesting by giving in to temptation and procuring one of the top-shelf magazines. But on this occasion, for him and my sister the level of embarrassment it caused would far exceed the usual.

Porn magazines in the 1980s were more of a skinny supplement than a bulky buy; with their wafer-thin spines they were really a pathetic excuse for a publication. And anyone attempting to remove one from the top shelf would bring another four or five magazines tumbling to the floor in a slippery mess that would eventually land wide open on a double-page spread of Samantha Fox. This is exactly what happened to the boy my sister was serving, who promptly turned a beetroot colour and tried to help my sister by collecting the half-dozen magazines from the floor and replacing them in their rightful position. The only problem was that if you weren't au fait with the correct way in which to arrange the skinny periodicals, the same scenario would simply repeat itself until the customer deferred to our skills of dirty-magazine arranging. The awkwardness then continued, as the lad realised he'd failed to fulfil the very errand he'd been sent on, and had to walk back into the shop to get the pint of milk. It was excruciating for him but a laugh a minute for us.

Truth be told, these magazines would have been better placed on the bottom shelf where less slippage was likely to occur. But it would have caused an outrage to place boobs and bottoms next to copies of *Woman's Own*, *Yachts and Yachting* and the *Country Companion*. It would be like setting up Maggie and Michael Foot on a date together. Never the twain shall meet.

Of course, if his levels of embarrassment were just too high, the boy could always pop over the road. With two shops on parallel corners, both owned by Indian Punjabi shopkeepers, it was inevitable that things would get tricky. Our own personal turf wars began around 1984 when the new shopkeepers arrived and lasted for the remaining time that we owned shop number two.

We had what most shopkeepers would consider to be the jewel in the crown – a newsagent's. The elegantly laid out broadsheets and tabloids would disappear within the first few minutes of trade and it always assured us a profitable income stream. Sundays in particular would see customers queuing around the block to get into our shop so they could get their hands on the meaty editions of news and supplements, then jump back into bed with a good cup of coffee.

It was on these days especially that we became well aware not only of a customer's political leanings, but also their choice of bedwear. When a shop is just a few minutes' walk away, there's no point coming by in your Sunday best. Our customers agreed, and all sorts of pyjama-wearing types would entertain us on a Sunday. Tartan pyjamas bought from Quality Seconds down the road, or mismatched tracksuit bottoms and a holey jumper – we had seen it all, but it was the Sunday footwear that would always bring about a surprise or two.

Magenta-coloured velvet soft slipper shoes with knitted pom-pom balls were popular among our female customers, while the men clearly had more time or the inclination to at least put on an old pair of trainers. But it was the customers who you could tell had thrown something on in a hurry, resulting in a combination that would never be seen outside a trip to the corner shop, who were my personal favourites. They cared little about what we thought of their fashion sense. But it would often result in them going arse about face when they forgot to fasten a buckle as they returned home clutching their copy of the *News of The World*.

Danger can creep in when you least expect it. And just because someone looks like you and has trodden the same path to reach the corner shop business, does not mean they can be trusted. As if Mum and Dad didn't have enough to deal with having to catch the school kids nicking our sweets, or keeping an eye on the skinheads at closing time, now one of their own was about to cause even more trouble in their carefully ordered world.

Our neighbour, the Asian shopkeeper, presided over a grocery store that sat on the corner of the street directly opposite. His was a slightly bigger shop than ours but did not have the benefit of selling cigarettes and newspapers. We referred to him in Punjabi as 'him next door'. Week after week he would watch with interest the queues of customers who would line the street waiting to buy their newspapers in our shop. It was this particular source of revenue that brought the green-eyed monster to these quiet suburban quarters.

We knew that something untoward was happening when our newspaper sales began to dwindle. 'Him next door' had taken it upon himself to assist with the queues that snaked around our street corner on a Sunday morning by selling newspapers in his own store, and he did so by unscrupulous means.

The two corner shop owners had never exchanged words before, but this was a situation that warranted a confrontation. Instead of walking some 20 yards to confront 'him next door', Mum and Dad decided to go one better and contact the hand that may have fed him the supply of newspapers. Newspaper wholesalers in the 1980s were in charge of issuing local licences to sell newspapers to newsagents all across the country. Just as we'd thought, the wholesalers had no knowledge of a new licence being issued to a corner shop across the road from us, and were just as interested as we were in finding out exactly how 'him next door' was managing to evade the licensing system and get hold of the Sunday papers.

The only way to determine what was going on was to peer through our net curtains and spy on the activities of the shop across the road. Bright and early, Dad played detective and watched as 'him next door' drove off at approximately 4.45 a.m. and returned fifteen minutes later with a car full of newspapers. Sally, the wholesalers' phone receptionist – with whom Dad was now on first-name terms – told him to continue with the mission and follow 'him next door' to work out exactly where he was going between 4.45 and 5.00 on a Sunday morning.

The following Sunday, Dad was up early to conduct his covert operation and surreptitiously followed 'him next door'. What he discovered was a betrayal of seismic proportions: our rival was getting his newspaper supply from another Asian shopkeeper a few miles down the road whom Dad knew and would always chat away with at the local cash and carry. Clearly this shopkeeper saw no harm in acting as the middle man to earn himself a tidy sum on the side for ordering double the number of newspapers he needed and selling half of them to 'him next door'.

When Dad relayed the results of his detective work to Sally, she wrote a strongly worded letter to the middle man warning him that his licence to sell newspapers would be revoked if he carried on supplying papers to unknown individuals. We had won – or so we thought.

If there's one thing a good shopkeeper is, it's resilient, so we had to take off our hats to 'him next door' for coming up with another way to snatch our Sunday customer base. We were informed by undercover surveillance conducted during lengthy gossip sessions in the cash and carry car park that another shopkeeper, also Asian, was willing to supply 'him next door' with a bundle of Sunday newspapers on the condition that he would drive twenty miles to pick them up. The idea of driving anywhere more than a mile away on a Sunday morning before opening time was madness, but 'him next door' was apparently willing to sacrifice his sleep to get a slice of our Sunday newspaper profit. Dad watched the car exit the street at 4.30 a.m. and return at 5.30 a.m. with a boot full of newspapers and clearly a new accomplice in this dirty war.

There was no point even attempting to track down the new middle man. We surrendered in this battle, knowing that Sunday trade from on now would be shared with the grocery store that was fast trying to become a newsagent on our turf. But all's fair in love and corner shop war, right? Mum and Dad thought it only decent that we provide our customers with a bit more choice, so they began to stock items that you might perhaps find in a grocery store. Within months of newspaper-gate, we introduced a few additions to our shop family. Eggs, bread and sugar arrived, then a wider selection of tinned foods and even the odd cucumber or two.

When the blows are dealt low you go lower. In 1983 our newsagents acquired a licence to sell alcohol; it was what we would call a 'ker-ching' decision, which undoubtedly made a dent in the takings of 'him next door' who had previously enjoyed exclusivity in the sale of booze. Lord only knows what the customers in the area were thinking. We would often spot our regulars, now spoilt for choice, making the most of yet another special offer that was advertised on the windows of the shop opposite. You can be sure, though, that we welcomed a lot of new faces through our front door too.

Muscle in on our territory and we'll muscle in on yours. The rivalry even trickled down to us corner shop kids, who despite playing a few feet away from one another did so in a strange environment of look, play but don't speak. Of course, what was happening on the shop floor was easier to track than what you couldn't see upstairs. The window of the bedroom I shared with my sister was directly opposite the bedroom window of the daughter of 'him next door' and, like some kind of forbidden romance, an unlikely and secret friendship emerged.

Only another corner shop kid would be eating their dinner after 8 p.m and would therefore be at liberty to exchange bedroom-window to bedroom-window evening banter. If a customer had happened to look up to witness these Asian girls holding up handwritten signs at their bedroom windows, ferociously using sign language to convey a message of urgency, they probably would have dialled 999 for fear we were being held against our will in rooms above a couple of corner shops.

We, the daughters of shopkeepers engaged in fierce competition beneath us, would use any prop, illegible handwritten note or animated signing to ask the same question over and over:

Me: *DO YOU LIKE ME?*
Daughter of 'him next door': *DO YOU LIKE ME?!*
Me: *Noooo . . . DO YOU LIKE ME?*

We were completely aware that we would be foolish to appear chummy when our parents were locked in a trade war. Our concern was maintaining a friendship through choice of hairstyles. To side ponytail or not to side pony-tail? If only life was always this simple.

With two Asian shopkeepers on opposite corners of a street, the work regime was crazy. But there were certain lines we wouldn't cross and the only two days off we had a year were to be protected at all costs. 'Him next door', on the other hand, cashed in on our inactivity and doubled his prices on Christmas and Boxing Day, knowing that he was the only shop trading in the area. To mark up your products by 50 per cent was a bold move, but a smart one nevertheless. Any customer walking through the shop door on a national holiday was in need of something and doubling its price would not deter them from parting with their cash if they desperately needed a loaf of white for the bread sauce, or a bottle of sherry for Nana's Christmas afternoon tipple.

Thankfully for us, not trading on Christmas Day didn't make a massive dent in the profits. Mum and Dad happily peered out of their windows to see the tumbleweed blow past our opposite number during the festive period. It turns out that people were more prepared for Christmas than 'him next door' would've liked. For us, to have two days off a year was sacrosanct, and no competition was going to sway our decision not to open up.

Every corner shop in Britain aims for a good profit margin, and knowing you're making money from decent mark-ups on your products can make the drudgery of running a shop worthwhile. 'Him next door' would regularly reduce the price of milk in an effort to steal our customers, but Mum and Dad would not be drawn into a battle on this particular item.

There was no point in fighting over spilt milk because the mark-up for us was minimal. It could be anything from 0.5 to 1 per cent and we preferred to keep our price the same rather than be accused by the customers of profiteering on an essential item whose price was set by government tariff. The nation had gone to war with Margaret Thatcher for scrapping free milk for children over the age of seven in 1971 as the then Education Secretary. Chants of 'Thatcher, Thatcher, milk snatcher' haunted her for decades and even fifty-odd years later, when the news broke of her death, the playground taunt reared its ugly head once again. It's a good reminder that if you mess with the nation's staple food supply, you will never be forgiven or forgotten.

In any case, there were plenty more items in our shop besides milk that would bring in the bacon. Like many a shopkeeper we abided by the Shaw's Price Book – a bible for corner shop owners, who could see at a glance a product's wholesale price and by how much we could increase it and set the profit margin. Profit on return would be calculated by the percentage margin you could make if you resold the product at the recommended retail price. There were, much to the delight of the shopkeeper, many items not listed in the book, in which case they were open to as big a margin as you desired.

It is no surprise that newspapers were the big earners. In the 1980s the print industry was thriving and the brutality of a 5 a.m. wake-up was quickly forgotten when you knew that for each newspaper sold in your shop you would see a 25 per cent return on sales. Sundays were even better, with a total profit of 40 per cent. We didn't care if you loved the *News of the World* or the *Sunday*

Times. As long as you continued to buy them from our shop, we were quids in and happy.

The mark-ups in a shop often dictate what you see when you first walk in and the last thing you cast your eyes on before you exit. We were particularly fond of pets and families in shop number two. Cat litter would be placed at prime position on the shop floor alongside cat and dog food, as these items would afford us a healthy 20–30 per cent profit. And no corner shop is complete without an array of family greetings cards. Whether it was an elephant holding a dandelion or a horse in a field with a pair of stirrups laid beside it, there was no better way to wish Granddad, or your sister, many happy returns of the day. Each card sold made us a whopping 50 per cent profit and we'd do our best to flog them at the till point when a customer's eyes would scour the shop landscape as they waited to pay for their goods. Product positioning was essential to the success of a business model known as 'bleed the customer dry':

Product	Profit on return (%)	Worth it?
Cigarettes	3-5%	Yes
Alcohol – spirits	5%	A constant winner
Alcohol – beer	20%	Especially on match days
Soft drinks	20%	Coca-Cola, Lilt & Cherryade firm favourites

Product	Profit on return (%)	Worth it?
Cat litter/pet food	20%	Woof woof!
Newspapers	25%	Obviously!
Sunday newspapers	40%	Who needs a day of rest?
Milk/bread & sugar	1%	Essential items bring customers in like bait – so yes
Eggs	18-20%	Poached or sunny side up?
Greetings cards	50%	Strategically placed by the counter as a must-buy
Sweets/chocolates	22%	Always
Frozen food	20%	For the boil-in-the-bag fish alone!
Ladies' tights	25%	Yes. Pretty Polly and Happy Shopper brands available.
Christmas decorations	80%	Potential for year-round sales!
Fireworks	20%	Must be sold within 10 days of permit date, so seasonal only.

With more than a thousand items in our shop, those on the list above are just a tiny selection. Another lucrative item, and one that was as popular as the newspapers, were the Football Pools coupons, which netted us a 12.5 per cent profit. These coupons were another advantage we had over the enemy across the road. But selling them was a service that required a great deal of time and attention.

The 'Pools Man' (as we called him) would come by the shop twice a week to collect all the Pools coupons and their takings. The supply of a Pools service was a good way of enticing a customer into the shop, but it required more attention than the simple stack and refill of most of our items. Mum and Dad would have to get all the documentation ready before collection day.

The full name of every applicant had to be filled out along with their address and the exact amount of money they had spent, so that if it was our shop that had sold the winning coupon, the customer could be easily traced. It was a task that Mum carried out meticulously as she didn't want to be responsible for a person not receiving their winnings. There was also the remote possibility that if one of the winning coupons had been bought in our shop, perhaps the winner would decide to share some of the jackpot with the dutiful shopkeeper who had written out their name so beautifully for years, week in, week out. Unfortunately we never did have a jackpot winner, but it didn't stop our family or our customers taking part in this national sport.

At its peak, the Football Pools was played by 10 million Britons in the 1970s and 1980s,[*] and for us it brought a steady stream of income and banter. It was a game the whole family would get involved with as parents dragged their kids into the shop to help fill out the coupons.

[*] 'Why I miss the halcyon days of the football pools', Michael Hogan, *Daily Telegraph*, 5 September 2014

Regardless of whether or not football was his or her sport of choice, everyone had a crack at this bit of low-level gambling. The simple cross-in-a-box exercise convinced everyone that they had a good chance of winning. Instead of trying to predict the football scores on a weekly basis, the customers would usually stick to the same numbers representing family birthdays or their kids' ages.

Dad, too, religiously filled out his coupon and it would join the hundreds of others that were stuffed into a large brown zip-up bag to await collection. The portly Pools Man would cart away a huge sack-load of coupons from the shop every Tuesday and Friday at 5 p.m. There'd always be a few customers rushing in at 5.01, breathlessly and desperately asking if the Pied Piper of the Football Pools world had been and gone. Never one to hang around, the Pools Man would have disappeared down a dark alleyway and would resurface only after the Saturday results.

An established afternoon ritual, the shop floor would always quieten down for an hour or so on a Saturday as customers rushed home to listen to the radio or switch on the TV to hear James Alexander Gordon read out the football results, his dulcet tones carrying with them the hopes and dreams of a nation. Conversations on the shop floor would typically revolve around the question: 'What would you do with the money if you won?' We heard many a tale from our customers, including dreams of buying an Aston Martin or flying Concorde to New York. Mum would jokingly reply, 'I'd have a day off,' a chuckle masking the fact that she was actually being entirely serious.

If 'him across the road' was pained by not being able to sell the Football Pools coupons, he could at least rely on a particular weekend of the year that was profitable for all Reading's shopkeepers. Every trick of the trade would surface when the August bank holiday came round and brought the hardened rockers of the nation to our doorstep.

The Reading Rock Festival in the 1980s was not all Eminem and Muse, as it is today, but a rock and heavy metal event that attracted headliners such as Black Sabbath and Iron Maiden to its main stage. Reading Rock was staged on the banks of the Thames across from the Caversham Bridge and a few minutes' walk away from our corner shop. It brought very hairy men who loved to drink to our side of town, and they took over this quaint Berkshire suburb for three full days of the year. Neither corner shop made any excuses for marking up the beers such as Budweiser and Carlsberg by as much as 50 per cent for the duration of the long weekend.

If any of us in the family had been seasoned rockers, which we weren't, we could have celebrated the fact that without paying a single penny for a ticket, we could hear word for word each rock band's session as if they were performing exclusively for us on a stage inside our little corner shop. Maggie may have heard angelic choral voices from the church opposite her bedroom window in Grantham, but over the years I heard The Kinks, Thin Lizzy and The Stranglers from mine.

The habits of a nation, whether they were gamblers or rockers, gave us the upper hand in the turf wars but I'm sure if you asked 'him next door' he'd query my account. Either way, it didn't matter as our corner shop became synonymous with success. It was a reputation that followed us into the cash and carry car park where, after years of custom, Dad was a respected face about town.

Just like the Pools Man collecting his coupons, trips to the cash and carry happened twice a week and Mum and Dad were a brilliant example of the teamwork required between husband and wife to successfully run a corner shop. Mum, who was the primary controller of all the stock in the shop, would carefully devise a shopping list for Dad that would mirror the floor plan of the large warehouses housing thousands of products for sale at wholesale prices. Mum's expert shopping list would ensure that Dad was in and out of the cash and carry with ample time to return home and help out on the shop floor. However, it did not factor in the time that Dad would take to smoke a cigarette and indulge in shop talk with the other shopkeepers while loading the car, which at times could last up to an hour.

When my sisters and I were in tow, we could report back to Mum that we obediently did our bit to help load the car while Dad was happily gossiping away to his mates. Every pair of hands could be utilised in the loading and unloading of a car, so we would devise a formation not unlike the rugby international players at Twickenham. Being the youngest, I was full back, tasked with carrying the lighter products such as toilet rolls and Kleenex Mansize tissues, which would usually end up last in the boot of our Volvo estate. But when natural development rewarded me with a growth spurt, I was soon upgraded to scrum half, handling beer cases and pet food.

Waiting in a car park for a trolley-load of goods, you soon become aware that you are not alone. Each car parked in this vast space told a story. Other children could be seen squabbling or playing 'I Spy' to pass the time. Mothers could be seen breastfeeding their children in the back seat, waiting for their husbands to finish stocking up on goods for a newly acquired shop. And elderly relatives would accompany their sons to the cash and carry just to enjoy a day out, even if it meant being stuck in a car park surrounded by metal trolleys and delivery trucks.

What us children all wanted, however, was the freedom to go inside. As soon as my twelfth birthday arrived, I became eligible to gain access to the inside of these, as I imagined, magical warehouses containing thousands upon thousands of products. Row after row of goods were piled high, from household detergents to cases of soft drinks and tinned food. And forklift trucks would whizz round the gigantic floor space, ready to help a shopkeeper reach the dizzy heights of a particular aisle. Here, everyone looked like us, and the cash and carry culture was to meet and greet fellow shopkeepers warmly while his or her kids (like us) ran riot.

Dad's face would quizzically examine Mum's shopping

list as he'd try to make up the time he'd lost gassing with his mates. He had little time to keep us all in check, as he'd be busy pushing a metal trolley that looked like a slab stolen from a mortuary from one aisle to another. It was much nicer to be inside than waiting on the outside, especially if the weather had turned. We could run around as much as we liked, and we did. Speeding past the washing powders and loo rolls, we'd race each other in the 800-metre-aisle race. We weren't the only ones. Corner shop kids who could've been picking leaves for a school project or enjoying their first kiss in the park were instead running up and down the aisles of a cash and carry before being brought up short by a security guard who was fed up of the deafening screeches of trainers skidding across the varnished floor.

The cash and carry chitchat was about more than escaping from the shop. It was a chance to gossip about other shopkeepers and, crucially, an opportunity to do business. In cash and carry warehouses across the land shopkeepers are cementing deals. It was perhaps during one of these encounters that 'him next door' found a willing accomplice for his elicit newspaper-selling. Dad, however, had much grander ideas than the petty ploy of dropping the price of a pint of milk by half a penny.

Local shopkeepers were hungry for bigger mark-ups on cheaper goods and Dad knew that if he could find a wholesaler that would do a deal on bulk buys then he'd be able to keep everyone happy (at a price, of course). The system of buying directly from the wholesalers gave shopkeepers a good base price and the ability to mark up generously to maximise the profit margins.

Dad figured out that you didn't need to be a supermarket to enjoy all the advantageous trappings of bulk buying. He suggested to many of the local shops that they come together and buy from the wholesalers in large quantities to keep their costs down. The suggestion was a success and Dad added a £2 per case cost for his efforts in picking up and distributing the extra stock. Suddenly a mandatory bi-weekly visit to the cash and carry became a nice little earner. For each trip Dad was making on average a solid £200, just for stacking the car full to the brim. As the amount of merchandise he was buying increased, Dad hurriedly replaced the family Volvo estate with a much larger white transit van, which he acquired from a biker who was advertising his pride and joy in the local classifieds. The van came complete with Bose speakers, a strange piece of cream carpet in the back and two large windowless back doors that made reversing it a game of potluck.

The cash and carry runs suddenly became more adventurous and my sisters and I would fight it out to get one of the two passenger seats in the front of this beast of a vehicle. The ten-minute drive would see at least one of us giggling for the entire trip as we sat perched high up in a position that gave us a wide-open perspective of the road ahead. With its badass sound system and colossal size, our van seemed to trample on all the other vehicles, which looked minute by comparison.

You can't really hide a huge white van from your neighbours, nor would we have wanted to. In turf wars, any blatant symbol of power can be used as a warning to back off or risk elimination. We were winning this battle, but a bigger one was on the horizon.

10

Sunday Bloody Sunday

'Sunday', noun: The day of the week before Monday and following Saturday, observed by Christians as a day of rest and religious worship and (together with Saturday) forming part of the weekend

In much the same way as a smoker plans his or her fag breaks at the office, a shopkeeper will split his or her day into key times. Any shopkeeper who sells sweets, chocolates and ice cream, for example, will tell you that school finishing time is a blessing and a curse.

Between 3.15 p.m. and 4 p.m. our shop resembled a stadium full of fans waiting to see their favourite pop star come on stage. Overexcited children between the ages of eight and sixteen would form large groups outside the shop to hang out and (in the summer) suck ice pops that would turn their tongues bright blue, orange or red, depending on flavour preference, or chomp away on a bag of sweets that within an hour would see them high from an intense sugar fix.

It was an intimidating scene and it would put off our older customers from coming inside the shop for fear of being brought down by a rugby tackle as they attempted to touchdown at the counter. It was also intimidating as a child when the only way to gain access to your family home was by navigating your way through a bunch of unruly kids. Hiding my embarrassment, I'd rush straight past the marauding group before Mum could put me to task helping her keep an eye on the chancers who shoplifted with varying degrees of success.

There are three ways to nick things from a corner shop:

1. Do it when the shopkeeper can't see you.
2. Conceal items cleverly beneath other items (namely magazines and newspapers).
3. Enter the shop immediately after school ends and divert the shopkeeper's attention with a load of scruffy teenagers.

The following are clear warning signs to abort a theft mission:

1. When the shopkeeper is prepared to whack you over the head with a wooden baseball bat concealed beneath the shop counter.
2. When they know your parents and will pay a visit to your home after trading hours.
3. When, in thirty years' time, you might bump into your local shopkeeper (now in retirement) and

will immediately suffer searing guilt and shame that will chew you up from the inside out and kill you almost instantly.

Mum knew which kids to keep watch over and imposed a strict regime at school kicking-out time to ensure the scrawny little shits did not overwhelm us. There is always a ringleader and once you cut them off, the others will quietly cooperate. A clearly written sign was pinned to the front door: 'One Child at a Time', a policy that I'm sure Chairman Mao would have approved of. The system worked and the kids would wait impatiently outside the shop door for their turn before sprinting in as if they'd been let out of a cage to run wild.

On more than one occasion fourteen-year-old Brett campaigned to buy cigarettes from Mum, and kicked up a fuss when she refused to serve him a packet of ten Silk Cut. Since Mum had watched Brett grow up, there was no way the now spotty, skinny teenager that stood before her could possibly convince Mum he was of the legal age to buy a packet of fags. She knew that he was fourteen years and 105 days old. Brett's offensive was stopped abruptly in its tracks when Mum said she'd be seeing his dad later when he came in to pick up a bag of spuds for their supper. Brett's parting statement, muttered under his breath, was: 'Please don't tell Mum.' She never did tell on Brett. I think that's why, whenever he now serves Mum at the checkout in the local Sainsbury's, he still feels indebted to her. Those 10p 'bags for life' do come in handy, especially when they're free.

Another frantic time of day was the morning rush hour, when a mix of regular customers would rub shoulders with passing trade at lightning speed. They'd come to 'grab and go' a packet of cigarettes, or a pint of milk, and almost always with a newspaper.

The daily 5 a.m. wake-up call to collect and sort the newspapers is perhaps one of the most taxing parts of owning a newsagent's. But as I've mentioned, what we lost in sleep was made up for in sales and the print industry was serving the shopkeeper well. Which paper a customer chose was the most obvious indicator of class and political leanings. The *Sun* was the best weekday seller in our shop but the weekends were a different story. Scores of *Sunday Times* and *Observer*s would give the *News of the World* a run for its money – all vying for the number one spot as the highest selling Sunday paper in our corner shop. Through newspaper choice alone, we learned much about our eclectic clientele. Sales of particular newspapers were also dependent on the seasons. Easter and summer breaks were when most of the *Sunday Times* and *Observer* readers were out of town. Their vacation time would put a dent in broadsheet sales and give the red-tops a temporary edge in the popularity stakes.

When the broadsheet readers returned, we would hear tales of what a wonderful time they'd had in Spain, which seemed the most popular destination for our customers who were enjoying the increase in the number of flights to the country after it entered the European Union in 1986. Taken with the Spanish lifestyle, they would inundate us with requests to supply a particular brand of Spanish wine so they could reminisce about their amazing holiday over a cheap bottle of Rioja and a bad attempt at home-cooked paella.

We always knew when the natives had returned as normal sales would resume on a Sunday, and for that we were grateful. The housewives of Caversham would push their husbands out of bed to go and collect the Sunday newspaper and this was our opportunity to catch a rare glimpse of the gentlemen we had heard so much about during the week. A bottle of Pink Lady or Babycham, or a box of Milk Tray chocolates to keep the missus sweet often accompanied their newspaper purchase.

Pink Lady was considered to be a luxury item in the 1980s. Positioned next to the more affordable Black Tower and Blue Nun, these wines were clumped together as they were the dinner party favourites. I was more taken by what was on the outside of the bottles than their contents, and would also examine the customers reading the labels as if they might deviate from their bottle of choice, but they very rarely did. You were either a Black Tower buyer or a Blue Nun.

With very little competition, since we were at least a decade away from the invasion of wines from around the world, the German brands dominated the market in the 1970s and 1980s. Black Tower was packaged to evoke the feeling of a castle estate but, to the touch, the dimpled bottle felt more like stroking a bumpy old lizard, and the glass was so black that you were forced to take on trust that the wine on the inside was indeed white. Blue Nun was our customers' favourite, as well as the nation's. At the height of its popularity, Britons were drinking a million cases of the stuff a year. I later discovered that it tasted like crap.

But it was at the bottom of the alcohol section that the best discoveries were made (or so I thought). The Babycham bottles were my favourite to look at. The small 200ml bottles sat neatly, although incongruously, alongside the beers on the bottom shelf. It was the only time I questioned my parents' merchandising decisions. Nevertheless, their position on the bottom shelf enabled me to replenish the stock that, to an eight-year-old's eyes, had an air of Hollywood about it. The image of a leaping deer on a bottle of sparkling wine might be bemusing to some, but for me it was a magical delight. The Babycham deer, surrounded by silver stars, looked as though it had just leaped off a Disney movie set. As far as I was concerned it was worth every penny for the opportunity to be close to a dancing Disney deer.

Years of watching the goings-on on the shop floor made me an expert at analysing social status, and I deduced that, aside from the purchase of a particular alcohol, the other strong indicator of social standing was hairstyle. Female customers with a disposable income would have one of two types of hairstyle: the Diana flick or the perm. The flick was a style created by sectioning out three pieces of hair from the front of your hairline and at either side above the ears. Each section was back-combed to create a triangle that reached proportions so high that the top-shelf magazines felt looked down on. The back and sides flick was championed by Diana, Princess of Wales and unfortunately, just like the home-cooked paella, it was achieved with varying degrees of success.

The perm was, in my opinion, a safer bet and it was my mum's hairstyle of choice. The process would usually take a mobile hairdresser around three hours to complete and it was the one luxury Mum enjoyed away from the shop. The hairdresser would leave the house, and us, smelling of ammonia for days and with curls so tight they would give Medusa's snakes a run for their money. Both the flick and the perm were evidence of someone who had the money and the time to look good, and no matter how drastic the outcome, all were welcome in our shop.

Sundays not only dragged the otherwise absent husbands out of bed, they also attracted a whole cross-section of random customers through the door. The extra hours in bed after the 5 a.m. weekday starts were savoured but Sunday was to become another working day – albeit a shorter one.

The decision to open up on a Sunday was an easy one. It was all about the money, and Sunday was one of the busiest trading days of the week. Anyone running a newspaper shop knew it. It's no exaggeration to say that on any given Sunday during the peak years of our business (circa 1983 to 1988), people would be queuing up to get inside the shop. Like us, thousands of corner shop owners reaped the benefits of Sunday trading and also exploited a loophole in a very unclear law.

The 1950 Shops Act required every shop in England and Wales to be closed on a Sunday except for the sale of particular products. It joins the draft Brexit Bill as one of my two favourite pieces of comic legislation. What you could and could not buy on a Sunday, according to the Shops Act, was outdated and bizarre:

- You could buy pornography but not a Bible.
- You could buy a G&T but not a box of tea bags.
- You could buy a fresh chicken but not a fresh egg.
- You could buy postcards but not a birthday card.
- A fish and chip shop could sell any dish on a Sunday except fish and chips. Other takeaways, however, could sell as much fish and chips as they liked – provided, of course, that they were not a fish and chip shop.

It was bollocks.

The act was riddled with so many anomalies that thousands of independent shopkeepers did not bother to take it at all seriously. Our decision to open up the shop between 7 a.m. and 2 p.m. on a Sunday was an extremely profitable one.

The morning task of sorting out the papers was much more arduous on Sunday due to their sheer thickness. Sunday magazine supplements arrived in a separate bundle and each one had to be painstakingly inserted into a newspaper by hand. It was a job that my mum loathed and she'd happily part with a few pounds for a couple of youngsters to do the chore instead. After about an hour they'd be done and would rush upstairs to scrub off the black ink that marked their hands and if left untouched could give you a fair idea of the newspaper headlines from the imprint on their palms.

Corner shop owners felt they could get away with half-day opening and cash in on the fact that the bigger stores wouldn't dare run the risk of such a flagrant transgression of the law and the resulting possibility of prosecution. They were right. But the law had also failed to account for a future that no longer bore a resemblance to 1950s Britain. Sunday – formerly a day of rest, a family day or a religious day – was already becoming very different.

The first ever football match played on a Sunday took place in 1974, when Millwall beat Fulham 1–0 at Millwall's home ground The Den in south-east London. The match signalled a big shift in what you could do on a Sunday. It was illegal to sell tickets to any football game on a Sunday but there were ways to get around the law. Organisers at The Den exploited a loophole by granting free admission to spectators on the proviso that each fan bought a programme before entering the ground. It worked, and the cost of a programme was the same as a weekday ticket. It was a sign of things to come. A commercial push to televise football without affecting match day attendance resulted in Sunday afternoon becoming a key time for televised games. Football paved the way for other sports, too. The men's final of the Wimbledon tennis championships, for example, has been broadcast live on a Sunday since 1982.

By the mid 1980s, the holy day had become a day of football, consumerism and indulgence. Dad said the speed at which customers bought their goods in the shop on a Sunday could be a sporting event in itself. It was worth a watch. Sunday trading was, in essence, carrying on the corner shop tradition of the last-minute rush to buy before trading hours were over. In the 1940s the corner shop would close on a Saturday at midday and reopen on a Monday morning. By the 1980s we were into seven-day trading and many a customer would run into the shop breathless on a Sunday afternoon to make sure they got what they needed by closing time. There was no doubt that demand would've warranted a further extension in opening hours, but 2 p.m. was set as a deadline so we could have at least five hours of uninterrupted family time each week.

The panic buying on a Sunday would last for the entire seven hours we traded, as customers would have no other place to go other than a corner shop for their emergency supplies. It served us well as the bigger stores stayed shut, abiding by the law, and we were thankful for the leg-up.

The Sunday trade, for small shops like ours, made up around 50 per cent of the weekly takings.

It was therefore a shock to find out that Maggie, the daughter of a shopkeeper, was desperately trying to transform the retail landscape in a way that would have a devastating impact on the corner shop.

11

Running on Empty

'Running on empty', phrase: To have exhausted all of one's resources

The guitar sounds of Status Quo and the thumping drums of Alice Cooper rattled the corner shop windows for one last time, signalling not only an end to the classic rock years of the Reading festival but also our time as newsagent proprietors. Mum and Dad got an offer they couldn't refuse to buy them out of the 'gold mine' that was shop number two, so they waved goodbye to 'him next door', a gruelling work regime and the magazines and newspapers that had dirtied their hands for six years.

A holiday, a newly acquired four-bedroom home and a new and exciting premises on the horizon . . . our fortunes were changing.

At last we had the longed-for doorbell, and it was a thing of beauty. With each ring came the promise of a visitor bearing gifts, or conversation. Either way I didn't care. It was a sign that we had come a long way. I would happily welcome an endless stream of Jehovah's Witnesses to our front door, just to hear the bell ring. As well as the doorbell, for the first time in my life we had a front door to a house that had a hallway, a kitchen, a downstairs toilet, a dining room and a living room. A staircase led to spacious quarters where I no longer had to share a room with one of my sisters. We had a bedroom each!

The views from the new house revealed the Reading skyline. From my sister's bedroom window you could spot the large octagonal building affectionately known as the Metal Box, which has recently been knocked down and replaced, and the Thames Tower that was once home to the global headquarters of the Swiss engineering firm Foster Wheeler. The far left of our vista revealed the large water tank on Mum and Dad's old stomping ground at cemetery junction. With this panoramic view of the town we were, it seemed, on top of the world. Who needed Manhattan when you had this? But it's a long way down when you are so high up.

It is a strange feeling to bid farewell to life above a shop. There was a comfort in the muted voices you heard while eating your lunch in the room beyond the counter service. You were never alone. Familiar faces would throw you a smile and tap you on the head as you tried to stock a shelf or two. We'd been desperate to get away, but the transition from corner shop to detached home was tinged with moments of nostalgia.

In a rare moment of privacy on moving day, I stood at my bedroom window in shop number two and whispered a prayer of thanks. I felt as though I was giving a solemn address at a wake. For the most part that shop had felt like a noose around my neck but I was clearly aware of the impact that those formative years would have on me in later life.

Still, there was not a single member of my family that was not giddy with excitement at the realisation we were moving. Finally we had a home sans shop, and a lifestyle to match. Our new, spacious abode was free of jarring noises from a commercial fridge-freezer. There was no mop and bucket in sight and on an average day there would be no more than five people walking in and out of our front door, all of whom were blood relations who were happy to wipe their feet on a mat in the porch (we actually had a porch!).

Mum and Dad were also now the proud owners of a garage and a large garden with a shed, three mature rose bushes, two apple trees, a pear tree and a veggie patch with its own runner bean trellis and fresh rhubarb. The lush emerald grass sprawled across two banks of lawn that were a joy to run up and down. It was like our own secret garden, and we were living out a dream in a home that was all ours.

Since the day I was born I had only known my parents as shopkeepers, so it took some adjustment to accept that there were other facets to their personalities. Who'd have thought that the pair of them were so green-fingered? A lifelong passion for gardening was finally given the opportunity to flourish as both of them would delight in pottering around the garden, planting seeds of runner beans, tomatoes and green chillies. Thanks to the hours and years of slaving away in the corner shop, Mum and Dad finally had the time to relax in a middle-class way.

If you looked closely enough, you might spot the unusual price tags on the pieces of furniture that adorned our new dwelling:

> *Garden furniture set complete with sun lounger and*
> *umbrella, paid for by optimum sales of greeting*
> *cards* ✓
> *Rear double-storey extension thanks to 312 days of*
> *sales of Sunday newspapers* ✓
> *One industrial-size lawnmower courtesy of countless*
> *Blue Nun purchases* ✓
> *Front driveway complete with side concrete pillars –*
> *cash and carry job on the side* ✓
> *My Little Pony notepad & pen, gift from customer* ✓

The decision to take a break after selling shop number two was an easy one. UK Competition Law dictated that all shopkeepers were prohibited from buying another shop within a three-mile radius for six months. For the first time in a very long time, a sizeable chunk of time was set aside for 'family and fun'.

Having never had a holiday since arriving in England in the 1960s, my parents decided the time had come for a lengthy family vacation. We could've gone anywhere ... Bermuda, Barbados or even Bolivia. Well, maybe not

Bolivia, which was suffering from a deep economic crisis and a flourishing drug trade. Instead it was decided that we would travel to the exotic shores of a far-flung place called Bournemouth. A bed and breakfast there was followed by a week on the Isle of Wight, which was tagged on as a spontaneous 'let's go because we can' holiday.

Despite the disappointment of not boarding a long-haul flight to sunnier climes, that holiday in the south of England remains a cherished memory. No Asian family takes a trip to the seaside without adequate supplies. Cheese and pickle sandwiches would be occasionally swapped for a packed lunch of Aloo Paratha (stuffed potato bread with spices), which we'd wolf down with a can of Coke and a delicious Cornetto for pudding.

We were, of course, still mindful of overextending ourselves, and being on a budget is the legacy of corner shop life. Everything boils down to money and now that the choice had been made to downsize, temporarily, to one income (Dad's) we could no longer rely on the cash generator that was the corner shop. Mostly what we did on holiday was walk, talk and eat – activities that required little spending. Mum would conservatively roll up her trousers, dip her toes into the English Channel and lament at how cold it was, while I waded past her to showcase my ever-improving front crawl.

On arriving on the Isle of Wight I lobbied my parents to buy me a glass tube filled with the twenty-one different coloured sands from Alum Bay. I was obsessed with having the souvenir after my sister had showed me one she'd got from a school trip to Shanklin Pier years earlier. I was green with envy and after a hard-fought campaign, I finally got my hands on a glass tube of multi-coloured sand. Packed lunches, swimming in the sea and munching on a stick of rock – this was our happy.

For the first time in my life, my mum was also doing what traditional mums did – picking me up at the school gates and keeping house. It took some time to adjust to. For years I had cultivated a meandering route home that allowed me to daydream wildly about the people passing by and reimagine their lives as if they were my own. Now a caring hand would grab mine for the walk home, rudely interrupting the freedom I had carved out for myself. What a time to decide you want to parent! Nevertheless, the touch of Mum's hand felt like a new beginning as we walked hand in hand to our new home.

We even got a dog, which I think meant that we were well on the way to achieving a middle-class lifestyle. The German Shepherd was called Raju – a Hindi word meaning 'king'. Raju had the most beautiful glossy coat of black and brown fur and was just as excited as the rest of us to be embarking on a new chapter in life. If he wasn't trying to hump my leg, he'd be busy getting under Dad's feet as he pottered around in the garden.

It was an edifying spectacle to have both parents around at the weekend. The sale of shop number two also coincided with no more night shifts for Dad and instead he enjoyed a nine-to-five, Monday-to-Friday week in a newly promoted role as supervisor at Mars. The only thing our perfect little world was missing was a white picket fence – and, apparently, another shop.

In the same way that my parents always knew that they wanted three children, they always knew they would buy shop number three. There are, however, some things you can't control when taking on a third baby, whether it be in human or shop form. Completing the family of five, they were blessed with yet another daughter. I've since managed to settle with them the question of whether or not they wanted me to be a boy. They claim they did not. But they were likely less fully prepared, despite years of perfecting their shopkeeping skills, for the set of circumstances that would unravel with shop number three.

Our third and final shop was the Rolls-Royce of convenience stores. The spec was as follows:

MODERN SELF SERVICE FOOD STORE/FULL FREE OFF LICENCE EASY 5 ½ DAYS
Occupying an excellent position in a parade of shops with good parking facility, servicing widespread and extremely pleasant residential area with the likelihood of 500 further homes being built in the close proximity on the outskirts of the prosperous Berkshire Thameside Town of Reading.

We are advised that takings over the last years have shown a growth of some 9%. Books and Accounts showing Gross Profit of 20.15% are available for inspection.

The final part of the legal document read like an invitation to Cinderella who must go to the ball. The contract read like a roster of achievements. The end-of-parade premises comprised a double-fronted shop with separate entry and exit doors, a delicatessen unit, two checkout points (for busy periods) and covered an impressive depth of 45 x 19.6 square metres. Mum and Dad knew exactly what they were doing when they bought this grocery store in 1988. The words 'easy trading' flashed before their eyes and were liberally used throughout the document, often written in bold and/or underlined for extra drama:

> _Easy hours_:
> _8.30 a.m. to 1 p.m. and 2 p.m. to 6 p.m. (6.30 p.m. Friday)_
> _Closed all Sunday, half day Saturday_

This shop was trading on almost half the hours of our previous shop and came with two part-time assistants and an array of gadgets and glossy furnishings. Shop number three created the same feeling for Mum and Dad as a doorbell did for an eleven-year-old: a sensation of euphoria, a feeling of joyful butterflies fluttering wildly in the pit of their stomachs.

The fixtures, fittings and utensils of this shop were beyond expectation. We had wire-mesh baskets the like of which were found only in the bigger food stores. And for those wishing to do a bigger weekly shop, a shopping trolley was available on request. An Asoli ham cooker stood proudly at the back of the shop, gleaming with a desire to impress the new owners. Not wanting to be outdone, the Berkel bacon slicer was even larger and sat opposite a walk-in cold room which lent the shop a 'wow' factor and would later become an overly familiar place to me for unfavourable reasons.

The mini superstore also had a Sharp electronic till and two pairs of scales, which Mum jokingly said would come in handy should one accidentally break (motioning in my direction and clearly not forgetting my expensive mistake as a six-year-old). This shop was so big it even had office space, a WC, a preparation area and a garage. The space above the grocery store was rented out and Mum and Dad had no interest in attempting to lay claim to it. They had been there and done that and now it was time to commute to work and distinguish between the two realms of work and play.

Since the shop was considered to be within walking distance of our secondary school (which, annoyingly, it was) we were still expected to help with opening up. Three helpers had become two, however, as my eldest sister was now at university. She had chosen a university that was more than a three-hour drive away, which according to her meant frequent trips home were too expensive. She was the first one of us to use this 'get out of jail' card, leaving behind a brace of siblings desperate to emulate her escape.

Being woken up at the witching hour was a thing of the past. The 8.30 a.m. opening time was kinder on all of us and thankfully was not subject to change. Under new ownership, a shop's trading hours can be shortened or extended at the whim of the shopkeeper. But thankfully in the case of shop number three we only added an extra hour to weekday trading (8.30 a.m. to 7 p.m.) and Saturday was no longer a half-day but a full day of service until 6 p.m. In comparison to our previous shops, however, this was a leisurely stroll in the park. Or so we thought.

The previous shop had been built on passing trade and newspapers, but shop number three had a very different model for success. Just as titty mags were an unfortunate staple of the old shop, so the new shop had an unpleasant mainstay that Mum had to get to grips with – slabs of raw meat. Between them, Mum and Dad had notched up a few jobs since they'd arrived into the United Kingdom – aspirin packer, spray painter, factory chargehand, parent ... but never butcher. But this mini market, which even had custom-designed headed paper for customer notices, had a regular and loyal clientele who for more than three decades had enjoyed the copious selection of meats that were on offer in a large delicatessen unit at the back of the shop.

We were now in charge of a convenience store that was a butcher, off licence and grocer's shop all in one, seemingly stepping back in time to the 1950s model of a corner shop where, once again, we were more than just a friendly face behind the shop counter. The speciality foods market had just started to take off, but our customer base was far removed from the trends of the day. Sales of Iberian ham or Gouda with cumin were still some years away for our patrons. The clientele of shop number three might as well have come straight from an old people's home. Around these parts, the cheese of choice was good old English Cheddar and a baby gammon joint was the preferred meat. This soon became a family favourite in our house, too, with the leftovers Dad would bring home. With the exception of Mum, we would do as the natives did and tuck into a gammon steak decorated with a pineapple ring and a fried egg on the side.

A Hindu vegetarian, Mum had to quickly overcome her morals and get to grips with life working behind a delicatessen counter. She also had to step up at meat delivery times if no one else was about to provide access to the cold store that would welcome the half-cut bodies of pig and joints of beef or lamb. Mum preferred to be nearer the front of the shop among the Battenberg cakes and Viennese whirls. Thankfully, Dad or one of the shop assistants was likely to be around but, if required, Mum would always take one for the team without a fuss.

Sacrifices were made by all of us. If it hadn't been bad enough walking past the marauding kids outside the corner shop, now they had to see me dressed in a matching skirt, jumper and blazer on a longer route to my secondary school from shop number three. My eyes remained firmly fixed on the pavement to avoid any possible eye contact with the kids walking uphill towards the local comprehensive while I travelled in the opposite direction to a private girls' school. In the six years of feeling embarrassed that finances had afforded me a different daily walk, it never got easier, but with each passing year I became emboldened by the sense that soon, I'd be outta there.

Each shop brought its own unique set of circumstances and dangers. The newspaper bundles had had the potential to slice the top of your finger off with their lethal tape, but in this shop the wide blades of the slicing machine could cut off your whole finger in one clean swipe, or, far worse, snap it tight in a fierce crocodile clinch and refuse to let go. The meat and cheese slicer was the Rambo of the utensils world. Stamina and strength were needed to operate the machine, with one strong arm turning the large metal handle that governed the two metal blades, while the other arm would guide a section of meat back and forth through the trap doors of this mighty piece of equipment. Any margin of error would result in a bloodbath, the potential loss of a limb and the costly waste of a decent cut of meat. Fortunately the shop came with two wonderful, dedicated members of staff who were up to scratch in the practice of meat-slicing and machine wizardry. They knew how to avoid spilling blood on the shop floor and how to retain all your fingers and thumbs.

A hazard that wasn't averted was a fifteen-year-old sister playing cruel jokes on a younger sibling. The walk-in cold room was a space that Dad proudly showcased to friends and relatives, who would come by to check out how our shop empire had evolved. With a regulated temperature of below four degrees, the room was accessed by a heavy-duty door with a giant handle that squeezed it tightly shut with the promise that nothing could get in or out. Its vault-like exterior revealed an altogether boring inside with rows of thin wooden panelled shelves waiting for meat and dairy produce. Things only really got interesting when the cold room was full of something, dead or alive . . .

The cold store had an unpleasant smell of ageing cheese and raw meat. It was fine for dead things but not for a thirteen-year-old who was led inside by her older sister who then slammed the door shut. These moments of cold-store trickery have joined my enduring childhood memories of 'For Mash Get Smash', the 'Secret lemonade drinker' jingle and Enoch's reference to 'wide-grinning piccaninnies'. There are some things you just cannot forget. Once trapped inside the dark cold room, I would try and stay as still as possible to avoid bumping into the body of a pig that was hanging from the ceiling above. My sister's laughter on the other side of the thick door would greet my screams of 'LET ME OUT!' Dad would eventually intervene and pull the door open to release me into the pure air and light. I'd hurriedly wipe away any visible tears and move on to plotting my revenge. There was, I thought, little justice in the world when we both got scolded for such antics.

But you don't always get what you deserve. And seeking fair treatment does not always mesh well with shop life. We were all reminded of the lesson in a stark way very early on with shop number three. The previous owners had shared details with Mum and Dad of their concerns about stock going missing from the alcohol section, which was at the back of the shop. Once they took over the premises, Mum and Dad were quick to rearrange all the merchandise and decided that they would move the entire off licence area to the front of the shop near the cash register to keep an eye out for any wandering hands.

It took an entire weekend of de-shelving and repositioning hundreds of bottles of wine, spirits and beer onto brand new ten-feet-long shelving that my parents had strategically placed near the shop's entrance. But in the time it took to take a step back and admire the fruits of our labour, the entire lot came crashing down, only just missing my sister who came within inches of having several bottles smash into her head. Mouths ajar, we stood silent and motionless with shock as puddles of smashed glass, wine and whisky started to form around our feet. More than a thousand pounds worth of stock had been destroyed within seconds.

The next twenty-four hours were spent vigorously clearing up the liquid and the shards of glass so that we could try and recoup the losses and open to the public on a Monday like nothing had happened. But for Mum and Dad, this incident would forever tarnish the excitement of opening up a new business – which, it turned out, would be our last.

By the mid-1990s, the customers were fading and shop life was beginning to resemble an old people's home. The number of regular customers who had relied on Mum and

Dad for their annual Christmas turkey and supplies of fresh sausages and bacon was beginning to wane. Having their customer base diminished by death was not something that my parents had accounted for when they eyed shop number three as a potential business. The passing trade that we'd so enjoyed in shop two was now passing us by too. The shop was part of a parade situated at the end of a very long road that was far removed from the hustle and bustle of a street corner. And the faithful customers who enjoyed a chat and spending a healthy amount on their weekly shop were leaving this world one by one and taking their business with them.

Of course, we chose to stick to the previous regime of not opening up on a Sunday, but even if we had been open, we knew that the next generation of loyal shoppers were being lured in a different direction. Within three years of us taking over shop number three a Tesco superstore had opened up two miles away, the third supermarket to now be operating in the area. Not content with six hours' trading time on a Sunday, the bigger stores invented a concept to coincide with the change in trading laws in 1994 called 'browsing time', which was guaranteed to attract a generation of customers who were fast becoming consumer addicts.

Trading time in a shop, according to the law, begins when goods are bought and sold, it does not begin when a foot crosses the threshold of a business. So as well as stealing our customers and stamping on the heart of small businesses, big supermarket chains realised that they could get a head start with their customers. By allowing them to enter a shop thirty minutes before trading time, the supermarkets gave customers time to browse all the goods that he or she would like before they were legally able to part with their pennies and pounds.

The thirty minutes of browsing time does not prohibit customers from selecting items and conveniently placing them into their shopping trolley. Nor does it stop them from casually parking the now full-to-the-brim trolley next to a cashier and indulging in a lengthy chat about the weather, and before anyone has had the opportunity to glance at his or her watch, time has miraculously passed and the cash register is legally open for business. Thus in the 1990s a new form of Sunday retail etiquette was born, which continues to this day, with people flocking to shopping malls, food stores and DIY shops that open thirty minutes before the tills do.

Sunday mornings for us had become about lie-ins and dog walks, but for others it was an opportunity to catch a good bargain away from the prying eyes of the local shopkeeper. Dad would spot many of our customers heading for the Waitrose or Iceland down the road, and they could barely look him in the eye. Sensing a need for further interrogation, our reliable dog Raju would abruptly seek out the traitors. 'Fancy seeing you here, Mr Sharma . . . what a lovely dog!' The greeting was made through a weak smile and gritted teeth, as Raju would vigorously attempt to sniff the customers' nether regions as they danced about him in a jig of shame.

The customers weren't the only quislings. Once upon a time, the local shop and the independent petrol station bumbled along together side by side without a care in the world – until the lines started to blur between us. The turf wars we engaged in with shop number three were against an old compatriot who had made a surprising entrance onto the battlefield. The humble corner shop is a place that feeds a nation. The petrol station, on the other hand, gets a nation moving. One sells food, booze, newspapers and cigarettes while the other provides fuel and car accessories. There was no contest to be had here. But the growing dominance of the supermarket in Britain was putting pressure on all independent traders, and the petrol station was no exception.

Independent petrol stations had lost their advantage when the trading laws changed, pushing the boundaries for competition wide open. Just like the corner shop, they were feeling the pressure of a rapidly changing retail environment. Now walking the streets of Britain wearing gigantic bulldozer boots, the supermarket could happily take out a shop and a petrol station in one big fat stomp. Supermarket filling stations were emerging across the country, offering below-cost-price fuel to attract customers to their out-of-town sites. There was no way the independent petrol station could compete with the undercutting of their prices, unless of course they did something radical and underhand.

They wouldn't, would they?

They did. And suddenly everything got very muddy in the corner shop landscape.

Corner shop owners were forever reinventing their business model, taking on lottery machines or deli counters, and owners of independent petrol stations were hit by a thunderbolt of realisation: they no longer needed to rely on fuel, with its slim profit margins, as their main source of income. All they needed was a lifeline, just like the one that had been given to the corner shops of Britain when they took on an open-all-hours-with-anything-you-can-buy formula.

By the early 1990s the independent trader was immersed in all-out retail warfare where anything goes. Petrol stations didn't give a second thought to stepping on corner shop turf and stole our unique selling point. While filling up a car, a customer could now buy a pint of milk, pick up a daily newspaper, maybe a loaf of bread and a choice box of cigarettes – all inside the friendly local petrol station, without even stepping foot inside a corner shop.

The only thing that separated us was the corner shop's ability to intoxicate the customer with a licence to stock and sell alcohol but that too was about to change. By 1994 the retail association which represented 7,000 of 18,000 petrol stations in the UK had already started a case for an alcohol licence claiming that many sites were, in effect, general stores and should be treated in the same way as supermarkets.*

* 'Garages seek right to sell alcohol', Cyril Dixon, *Independent,* 18 December 1994

Retail life is a big roundabout of legislation and, as with the 1950 Shops Act, history would repeat itself by creating absurd laws that were open to abuse. The Licensing Act of 2003 states that petrol stations are prohibited from selling alcohol on site because they are primarily used as a 'garage' for the sale of fuel. However, if a petrol station can prove that it is not just a 'garage' and most of its custom is non-petrol, it can be granted a licence to sell alcohol. Chuck them a lifeline and they'll turn it into a pot of gold.

Within ten years of the 2003 Licensing Act, 3,000* petrol stations across Britain began selling alcohol. Each site had put forward a convincing argument that they were providing a genuine community service where a local shop or supermarket was absent. Cheeky gits. Surely the corner shop owners of Great Britain were the only ones who had the right to turn the nation into fervent smokers and alcoholics with bad taste in newspapers?

Even a couple of decades before the corner shop's independent monopoly on alcohol was ended, with three supermarkets in the area, and a petrol station supplying milk and newspapers around the corner, our shop was struggling. All we could do was batten down the hatches, hope for a miracle and do what the British do best. Anyone for a cuppa?

---

* 'Alcohol and petrol stations, Sibelius software, car insurance and Nespresso' *You and Yours*, BBC Radio 4 (24 August 2012)

12

The Customer Is Always Right

'The customer is always right', saying: To emphasise in business that it is very important not to disagree with a customer or make them angry

We, the corner shop families, are the custodians of a vault filled with secrets about you and yours. Throughout the years in shops numbers one, two and three, there was a common thread that bound them all – the customer. Corner shop life would be grey indeed without the animated characters that walked through our shop door every day. Each brought with them colourful stories they chose to share with us, and in turn we became part of their narrative.

The shopkeeper–customer bond from Maggie's father's day to now remains unaffected by the passing of time. There is an invisible contract between the server and the served – the server should never ask questions or divulge information, unless of course it's within the confines of the corner shop family home, in which case we'd gossip frantically about what had happened on the shop floor earlier that day. At what point the line between shopkeeper and counsellor begins to blur is hard to know, but he or she occupies a privileged position that requires great care. We are dealing with sensitive information about the personal lives of our customers. And the daily encounters and habitual purchasing of a product can reveal more about a customer and their innermost feelings than an hour-long conversation.

She walked in with bruises as purple as Quality Street all over her legs. We were told it was an accident, but after years of serving her a bottle of vodka every day, we knew Mrs Cross was a dipsomaniac. A retired teacher, she'd hit the bottle hard when her husband died of a heart attack in the early 1980s. The bottle-a-day habit would dull the aching loneliness she felt and became a constant companion in her otherwise solitary life. We of course obliged her addiction by receiving her monies, but the long conversations that followed across the counter in shop number two were on the house. It was part and parcel of being a shopkeeper. Our shop was in the heart of the community and that meant it wasn't just material goods we were providing. Mum never considered the hour-long chats a chore, even if Mrs Cross's words were as shaky as her wobbly knees. Whether they were young or old, rich or poor, clean-living or debauched, we would never judge our customers: all were welcome in our shop, which at times resembled a shelter for the needy.

We had nobility among us too. One of our most profitable customers in shop number three was a Lady Barford, who would travel some eleven miles to our premises for her fortnightly shop. Lady Barford lived in a beautiful house on the banks of the River Thames in the village of Sonning, long before it became famous for its A-lister residents such as George Harrison and George and Amal Clooney.

Star status was afforded to this loyal customer who had been a long-standing patron of the previous owners and remained dedicated to the shop for the entire time we owned it. Lady Barford spent at least a hundred pounds every two weeks in our shop, and her purchases reflected the aura of wealth she elegantly wore like a cloak. By the way my parents greeted her, you'd think the Queen herself had come among us. I could only observe these interactions with amazement and wonder. Was this how the Indians had exchanged dialogue with nobility during the time of the British Raj in India? For her part, Lady Barford was pretty down to earth and seemed not to notice the red carpet treatment that was laid on for her on a fortnightly basis.

Lady Barford's entrance to the shop was a grandiose affair. Steady on her feet for a seventy-six-year-old, she'd walk in commanding attention. And waving her walking stick as if she was about to magically pluck a rabbit out of a hat, it would miraculously unfold into a sturdy folding chair and a temporary place of rest. The chair was then carefully and strategically placed next to the shop counter, so that she had a full view of the entire shop and its contents. During the winter a worn tartan blanket strewn across her knees would accompany the folding chair. What then followed was our very own version of *Supermarket Sweep*.

From her central viewpoint of the entire shop Lady Barford would shout out items from her shopping list and watch Dad move from aisle to aisle as he'd obediently follow her instructions. The two had an affectionate bond and Dad would often play silly as he walked past the row of strawberry jams for a third time to get a laugh from their loyal customer, while his wife wondered if he had genuinely forgotten that they'd moved the jams from the middle section last week to make way for the arrival of the tinned treacle sponge puddings.

Lady Barford would then enquire as to how all the family were doing, which was Mum's opportunity to boast about how all three daughters had been privately educated at the local girls' school, with the eldest away at university. Lady Barford would nod in approval before being side-tracked by the twelve rashers of streaky bacon that were being sliced for her. A driver would wait patiently for Lady Barford as she carefully cross-checked her shopping list with every boxed-up item before Dad would help load them into her car. The visit would last approximately sixty minutes including pomp and circumstance, which we all enjoyed – along with the fortnightly spend, of course.

There are very few places in the world where all ages, social classes, ethnic groups and political viewpoints can occupy the same space for a moment of time. With Lady Barford exiting shop right, Shelley would walk in the front door shop left and exploit the kindness with which my parents greeted every customer who shopped in our store.

Shelley: 'I'm so sorry, Mrs Sharma, I forgot my wallet – is there any chance I can come back in tomorrow and pay you? Please, I really need this shopping. Please?'

Mum: 'Well we wouldn't normally do this, especially for cigarettes and alcohol, but I suppose you can ... Definitely tomorrow – you'll come back at 4 p.m.?'

Shelley: 'Of course, Mrs Sharma!'

Off Shelley went with two large bags full of shopping that totalled some £50 in Benson and Hedges cigarettes, Heineken lager, Andrex toilet roll and a variety of tinned foods.

She never did turn up the following day to pay it back, but it was an error of judgement on her part to think that she could get away with it. Dad in particular was livid at the lack of respect this customer had shown when we had done her a favour out of the goodness of our hearts. It was one IOU that he was not willing to dismiss. We knew everyone's addresses in the area but Shelley had clearly thought her plan through, as two days later, when Dad knocked on her front door, he was alarmed to hear that

Shelley no longer lived at the property. Deceitful, thieving lowlife – Shelley had done a runner.

As Dad turned to leave, the new tenant motioned him back and in a stroke of good fortune said, 'I think I have a forwarding address for her if you want it?' Dad could not have planned the chain of events that followed any better.

Dad's victory was within touching distance, but there was one small problem – the address he'd been given lacked the exact number of the flat this single mum with three children now occupied. It was a small obstacle, however, which Dad believed could be easily overcome. There are three fifteen-storey high-rise blocks in Reading's Coley Park that stand out because of their pale pink paint that to this day commands attention for being such a random choice of colour for blocks of council flats. Dad didn't know which block or number Shelley was living in, but he decided that he would get through all the flats, no matter how long it took to find her. If word got out that Shelley had 'got away with it', the floodgates would open for other fraudsters to take the piss too. Such precedents for bad behaviour would not be tolerated in our shop.

Going off to teach Shelley a lesson turned out to be quite convenient. The blocks of flats housing their debtor were near a cash and carry on the west side of town. Mum and Dad decided that if it took weeks or months to find her then they would not use up petrol unnecessarily, but instead get a job done at the same time as taking it upon themselves to police the community.

There are moments in a shopkeeper's life where you

look up at the skies and thank a special power for small mercies. The hours of backbreaking work are often rewarded in the most unusual ways. Dad rang the doorbell of the first flat he came to, and, as if he had won the Football Pools jackpot, Shelley popped her head round the front door. She was completely dumbfounded by the sight of this Asian man who had brought his whole family in the back of his Volvo estate to her council flat to see how she was getting on a week after doing a runner from our shop. The blood drained from Shelley's face with the realisation that she had been caught out. A flurry of sorries engulfed Dad, who was now in a state of shock that the culprit had been so quickly and easily found.

Shelley promised to pay back every last bit of the money she owed and hurriedly searched her tracksuit bottoms for change to hand over on the spot. The fiver she gave Dad would do in the interim, but rules were rules and Shelley knew that it was imperative that she find a way to pay back the outstanding debt, and keep this dogged Asian shopkeeper at bay. After a few minutes of grovelling, they made an agreement that Dad would pass by Shelley's flat every week on his way to the cash and carry and collect whatever monies she could afford to give at the time. We were in no rush for the debt to be repaid but it was in Shelley's interests to get rid of Dad as quickly as possible. With a verbal contract agreed, Shelley shut the door and a chorus of expletives could be heard emanating from her flat. It was a day of reckoning for

Mum and Dad and an incident that Shelley was unlikely to forget. Within four weeks the debt was cleared and Mum and Dad revelled in the small victories that corner shop life can bring.

Of course, it's a two-way street, and as a shopkeeper – or a shopkeeper's daughter – you don't really have the option of living a life of obscurity either. It was a lesson I learnt the hard way.

The walk home from school was approximately 0.3 miles and according to Google Maps in today's world it would take six minutes. But since my legs liked to meander while I daydreamed, my nonchalant trek back to the shop took at least fifteen minutes. I paid little attention to the Green Cross Code as I zigzagged the streets on my way home. Crossing the road in between two vehicles was the biggest no-no in the rule book of road safety, but the benefit of hindsight is a wonderful thing. Darting into the road like a meerkat, I ran into a blue Ford Fiesta whose bumper met with the left side of my body and momentarily winded me as all the breath of my eleven-year-old body was knocked out of me.

Realising the seriousness of the mistake I had made and not wanting to get in trouble, I ran straight through the shop door and up the stairs to scour the scene from the privacy of Mum and Dad's bedroom window. Here I had a front-row view of the entire road and watched the driver of the vehicle I had just collided with pull over to the side of the street. He then got out of the car and walked into the shop.

There are nooks and crannies in a shop that are only found during games of hide-and-seek and are usually reserved for the younger members of a corner shop family. The far right corner of my parents' bedroom housed such a find. The gaps between the worn floorboards were far enough apart to peer through with one eye at the goings-on of the shop floor. They also provided my sisters and I with hours of fun when we were living above shop number two, as we'd shout out, 'Can you hear me?' from the cracked floorboards to the shop below, leaving the customer bewildered by the strange muffled voices they were hearing. On this occasion, though, I was using the floorboards solely as a listening device and with my heart racing, I desperately tried to catch my breath.

I could hear Mum ask the driver if he wanted a glass of water as she gave him a stool to sit on behind the counter, before asking him what had happened. In a raspy voice, the driver explained how a young girl had just run out in front of his car and then sped into this shop, and he was desperate to find out if she was okay. If I'd had the energy to shout through the floorboards, I could have told him that I was doing just fine … up until the point that he decided to go public and inform my mum about our brief encounter. I knew then that I was in trouble.

I heard the distinctive squeak of Clarks shoes heading up the stairs looking for me as I rushed into my bedroom and pretended to be doing some reading. I feigned surprise at hearing the news of the driver's unfortunate meeting with my lower left abdomen. Preoccupied with being taken away from the shop floor, instead of asking me if I was hurt (which I wasn't), Mum clipped me round the ear and told me not to cause the locals any trouble.

Customer satisfaction was, and remained, priority number one.

The story of an immigrant family in a working-class community running a local shop brought together the most unlikely combination of people. In shop number two we were living on the same street as a GP, a builder, a teacher and a student, not to mention rubbing shoulders with the hundreds of people from all walks of life who entered our shop on a daily basis. We, the immigrant family, could have been part of a social experiment, planted like a tree to see how well we would take root and whether or not we would establish ourselves in new soil and mesh with the other foliage. We were, as Mum points out, very lucky. Simply being positioned in the centre of community life does not necessarily make you feel as if you are part of it. Becoming part of a non-biological family happens because of kindness and love, and we were fortunate to be showered with both by loyal customers who became good friends.

Owning a shop inadvertently gave us an extended white family who not only gave us their cash but spoilt us kids with gifts and the offer of a free childcare service which Mum and Dad made good use of. Customers were often on first-name terms with their local shopkeeper and they looked after their sprogs not because they had to, but because they wanted to. It worked both ways, though – there were members of our extended white family whom we held in great affection, and if they really needed something, we would do our best to oblige.

Mrs Fay was an elderly lady whose mobility was waning and her regular visits to shop number three had been replaced by ordering her goods over the telephone. The phone shop was time-consuming for us but convenient for her, and our gesture of goodwill was to offer a free delivery service to Mrs Fay after closing time. She became particularly fond of us corner shop kids and in a very Indian way suggested we call her Aunty Fay.

Aunty Fay could map out the shop floor and its contents like an expert player of *The Crystal Maze*. Her photographic memory meant that at times she knew the shop layout better than any of us. If we had decided to rearrange an aisle or two, Aunty Fay would want to know about it so she could get her shopping list in the right order as she recited the items aisle by aisle. In later years, however, the telephone calls became bittersweet as her once active and brilliant mind succumbed to dementia. What had once been a triumph of recollection had now descended into a game of 'Give Us a Clue'.

Not one to be beaten by brain disease, though, Aunty Fay never stopped trying and we all found other ways to decipher the contents of her shopping list. As brand names faded from Aunty Fay's memory she would depend solely upon the colours and images of an item. The onus was on Mum to come up with the goods, and the women would celebrate a small victory when, for example, Aunty Fay's description of a box with a woman wearing a sari in the fields led Mum to a box of PG Tips teabags. The two would laugh away on the phone, rejoicing in the drawn-out moments of success. It didn't matter how long it took to complete the telephone order of Aunty Fay's shopping list. For the fun we all had in playing the game, it was worth it.

Daydreaming behind a shop counter was the most peaceful way for me to pass the hours of shop work. Every customer would be subject to my scrutiny. Their run-of-the-mill visit to the shop was now perfect fodder for my teenage imagination, particularly when it was a shopper of the male variety. Being at the forefront of the community meant that in the afternoon you could be serving a Toffee Crisp to the very boys with whom you'd locked eyes on the school walk that morning. Payment could be by way of a smile and a wink if I was so inclined. Unfortunately, though, I wasn't really in a position to play the temptress. If I could have, I would have said 'This one's on me, love' while seductively stroking my hands across the orange wrapper, ensuring our fingers met briefly as the Toffee Crisp exchanged hands. But this never happened. How could it? Everything we said or did was open to interrogation. We were at the centre of community life and our lives were on public display.

Subtle references to the success of our empire would also surface during our daily transactions in shop number two:

Mum: That will be £2.99 please. Shall I cancel your *Country Homes* for the Easter break?

Customer: No thanks, we're staying home, catching up on chores and seeing the grandparents. I see the shop's doing well – private number plate on Mr Sharma's new Volvo now, eh?

Eh? What's it got to do with you and your monthly order of *Country Homes*? It was possibly a response that Mum would've liked to have given, but instead she smiled politely and handed over the magazine, albeit with its pages ever so slightly dog eared.

Anyone who wanted to gaze in on our lives could do so at any time. And they would see that Dad was a proud Volvo man. The cash and carry car parks were strewn with Mercedes Benzes and BMWs, exhibiting to the world that the Asian shopkeeper was 'on the up', but for Dad the Volvo was the vehicle of choice. The bright blue X-reg with a front opening boot door was spacious enough to carry a carload of shopping and three kids and a wife. It was the king of cars, and practical for doing the large stock runs, but it wasn't long before the Volvo was used merely as a family car. A transit van would soon be acquired to take up frontline shop duties.

We enjoyed the Volvo experience most on a Saturday evening, when it came complete with family jokes and a bag full of sick. In the brief twenty minutes it would take Dad to drive from Reading to Slough to visit his sister, you could guarantee that at least one of his three daughters would be puking in the back seat. The anti-static rubber strip tagged to the car bumper was supposed to stop passengers from getting car-sick, but it did little to prevent the churning of our weak stomachs. Mum and Dad would try to divert attention from the saliva collecting in our mouths by sharing a classic family joke. The 'who farted?' joke would be met with raucous giggles and was perfectly timed to take in the waft of sewage passing junction 7 of the M4 as Dad explained how the town was called Slough because it literally meant shithole.

We had the car and the private number plate; something that didn't go unnoticed by our regular customers. But my parents had also acquired the skill of masking the truth. It was a trick that I had learnt from the best teachers of all. You can't expect a shopkeeper to always be genuinely happy to see you when they're working fourteen hours a day, seven days a week, but somehow my parents managed to paint a picture of harmony. In between blazing rows about the most mundane issues, serving a customer with a smile was of paramount importance. The cause of these arguments was usually something like Dad forgetting to collect the toilet rolls from the cash and carry, or Mum misplacing an invoice that needed paying. But to the outside world they were always beaming and their professional expressions revealed little about their private lives.

The customer, on the other hand, was more forthcoming in divulging any personal grievances or marital woes. The countless hours of gossip could get tiresome. 'Did you hear about the head teacher running off with the class-room assistant?' 'Ooh, Tony down the road was caught in a compromising position with another man in the precinct car park!' The best type of a customer for a corner shop kid is one that can make your innards ache from laughing so hard. Arthur was such a man and, as was the custom, he succumbed to the title of 'Uncle'.

Uncle Arthur was a portly man who always wore the same clothes: a fetching knitted tank top, a white shirt, and braces that held up oversized trousers. These items varied only in colour, and he wore them year round; if the weather turned, he'd add a splendid black bowler hat and raincoat. But whatever the weather, the elements would not sway him from his daily excursion to shop number two. His routine would involve a morning visit to collect the newspaper, then he'd return later in the day to buy a copy of the local paper, the *Evening Post*, which would arrive at 5.30 p.m. The evening sojourn would last around two hours and the counter's edge was the perfect spot for a good natter. He would stake out his position until clos-ing time before doffing his hat and bidding us all a good night's sleep.

Uncle Arthur became as regular a fixture in the shop as the rows of shelving that lightened the load of a heavy burden. He was a guardian angel of sorts. Mum relaxed a little during the evening hours when she knew he was around. With one arm propped against the jar of sweets and a hip leaning against the freezer chest, he'd only move when a customer was in need of a particular item that was being blocked by his six foot four inch frame. He'd goad the customer into buying something that was on special offer and wink at Mum when another sale was put through the cash register. His banter was worthy of its own primetime spot on national television.

As the years passed, we realised that we were his saviours too. Now retired, his days of serving as a soldier during the Second World War were long forgotten. It was his twice-daily visits to our shop that gave structure to his day. A widower with no children, we were Arthur's family and for every day that he kept a watchful eye over Mum during the late hours of cashing-up time, in turn we did our bit to relieve him of his boredom and loneliness.

The customers expected to see Uncle Arthur as much as they expected the 1kg bag of cat litter to be on special offer. He was one of only a few who understood what our world was all about. His presence on the shop floor was irreplaceable.

Arthur also had the shopkeeper's skill of concealment. Once he walked out of the shop door we knew little about the life he led or the home in which he lived. Corner shop banter didn't reveal the extent of his isolated existence. Uncle Arthur died in 2004 and after his death we glimpsed something of his life through the terraced house that he had occupied for decades.

Much like Maggie's family home in Grantham, Arthur's house had an outside toilet, but never once had he complained about having to traipse to the loo at the bottom of the garden. A 99p tub of Brylcreem and a pocket-sized comb were the last visible signs of our ties with Uncle Arthur – items he had bought in our shop that revealed little of the long-standing friendship we had enjoyed. He departed this world leaving behind a kindness you cannot buy and a heart full of precious childhood memories.

13

Shutting up Shop

'To shut up shop', phrase: To close business at the end of the day or permanently; to become defensive or inactive

Seven miles east of Belfast city centre is where you'll find the Carruth family corner shop. The original shop was built in 1889 and eighty years later it was dismantled and moved brick by brick to a model village. You can see the Victorian building in all its glory at the Ulster Transport and Folk Museum in Belfast, which has lovingly preserved it. You can buy sweets from old-fashioned glass jars and admire the limited supply of post-war goods on offer. Clearly the Irish had enough respect for a time gone by and a family tradition to want to lock it into history for future generations to enjoy.

Unfortunately none of the three shops my parents owned would qualify for preservation in a quaint museum. Shop number one near Cemetery Junction is now an unremarkable residential property. The occupants are probably completely unaware that their home used to be a complete shithole until Mum and Dad gutted it to make it a half-decent place that would welcome thousands of strangers through its front doors. Shop number two – the gold mine – is still a retail space, but of a very different kind. Caversham has continued to set itself apart from its neighbours, attracting socially mobile families who see the area as a desirable place to raise kids. Our old shop is now a hair salon for children. Residents clearly have plenty of disposable cash to sustain a 'kids only' hair-dresser to tend to the locks of their precious little ones. As for shop number three, it sold its soul to the franchise market.

Shutting up shop is usually down to one of three scenarios:

- Forced closure due to falling sales
- Bankruptcy
- The end of the family line

By 1996 we were by no means bankrupt, but with far fewer customers and no one else willing to take the reins, the writing was on the wall. It was also due in part to Maggie, the shopkeeper's daughter who had once upon a time accompanied her father on delivery runs and served customers, but now turned her back on where she came from. Despite her repeated attempts (twenty-six to be exact) throughout the 1980s to repeal the Shop Bill in Parliament the Sunday trading laws had still not been relaxed. However, if at first you don't succeed, the twenty-seventh time might just hit the jackpot.

The Sunday Trading Act was passed in 1994 across England and Wales and in much the same way that the supermarkets had done thirty years earlier, it stuck a giant nail in the coffin of the corner shop. The Act governed the rights of shops to trade legally on a Sunday. It said that shops over 280 square metres:

- Can open on Sundays but only for six consecutive hours between 10 a.m and 6 p.m
- Must close on Easter Sunday
- Must close on Christmas Day

Goliath had been waiting for this moment. For more than a decade he had watched David enjoy the fruits of his labours illegally, but now it was time to share the fun, and David was about to be dealt a blow of gigantic proportions.

In the same way we had enjoyed exploiting the loopholes of the 1950 law, the supermarket was about to do the same to us.

Having watched how the corner shops of Britain broke the law and got away with it, the supermarket was ready to launch a revenge of magnificent proportions. Not wanting to be limited to a mere six hours of Sunday trading, the supermarket decided it was time to create a hybrid.

The Sunday Trading Act of 1994 allowed smaller shops that measured up to and including 280 square metres to open their doors for trading at any time and on any day of the week. Rather cleverly, the supermarkets began to downsize to take full advantage of serving the British customer twenty-four seven, a tradition that had previously been reserved for the corner shop only. Mini-supermarkets began to pop up in prime positions at the heart of the community for 'convenience and ease'. Gone were the days of customers exclusively shopping 'out of town' on a weekly basis and the supermarkets knew it. They had seen how the corner shop had adapted its business model when it began its renaissance in the 1960s. And by plonking itself in a very visible spot on high streets up and down the country, the mini-supermarket could take full advantage of the spontaneous purchases, passing trade and emergency supplies that we had so brilliantly catered for.

MINI-SUPERMARKET: Ooh, fancy bumping into you here!
CORNER SHOP: F*** off.

Like a wolf in sheep's clothing, these 'little' stores belonging to big names in the supermarket world started appearing all over the nation. Cosy words were added to their brands to imply that these shops were still local and would not trample on the identity of smaller shops but coexist harmoniously side by side. Liars. The words 'express', 'local' and 'little' disguised the mammoth corporations behind the smaller stores. The random shopper that had once walked through our doors was now being coaxed in another direction.

Campaigns and demonstrations by anti-Sunday-trading groups were fruitless, and placards arguing 'Don't give in to supermarket greed' and 'No government can change the laws of God' were discarded on the pavements of Westminster. Maggie, the daughter of a Methodist preacher, didn't exactly change the laws of God but I doubt even she could have predicted how shopping would become a new form of Sunday worship.

The new legislation did, however, grant one concession to the naysayers and still prohibited large shops (those over 3,000 square feet) from trading on Easter Sunday and Christmas Day (when it fell on a Sunday)[*]. But the rest of the year was wide open for retail exploitation and a new way of behaving on the traditional day of rest. The British Retail Consortium says Sunday is now second only to Saturday for footfall and total sales and is the busiest day of the week in terms of hourly sales. It's amazing how many shops you can get round when you know you only have a six-hour window to do it in. The Trafford Centre in Manchester, The Oracle in Reading and The Bull-ring in Birmingham are just a few examples of shopping complexes built after the 1994 law change. Today they benefit from millions of visitors every year.

---

[*] The Christmas Day (Trading) Act 2004 later made it illegal for large shops to open on Christmas Day whichever day of the week it fell on.

Even Maggie's old turf hasn't escaped the impact of Sunday trading. Across the road from 1 North Parade in Grantham, where the family's grocery shop once stood, now looms a large Asda superstore that's open from 7 a.m to midnight on Mondays, 6 a.m to midnight four days a week and 10 a.m until 4 p.m on a Sunday. We can thank the grocer's daughter and the thousands of other super-stores that open round the clock for sucking the life out of the corner shop.

The idea that these 'local' supermarkets are doing us a favour by being conveniently located on our busy high streets is a misrepresentation. We all pay an elevated price for such convenience, with some of the smaller stores charging as much as 7 per cent more for products than their larger supermarket counterparts. Apparently, running costs and rent are enough of a reason to hike up the prices without us knowing about it. Clearly we all have to pay a price for the demise of the local shop.

If this piece of legislation dealt a severe blow to the inde-pendent shopkeeper, another one was on its way. Twelve months after the 1994 Sunday Trading Act, Sunday licensing laws were also relaxed. From 1995 onwards pubs and other places selling alcoholic drinks were able to open as long as they wanted. Along with newspapers and cigarettes, alcohol was hugely lucrative for corner shops. It was a double blow in the space of a year – the law was digging a hole for corner shops to jump right into.

The only way a corner shopkeeper could survive was to try and stay in the game. If opening all hours of the day, seven days a week was the new tactic in a dirty war, so be it. But for us it was a step too far. Corporate competition had got the better of thousands of Asian shopkeepers. Between 1990 and 1998 7,000 independent shops disappeared* and in October 1998 we would become part of the statistic.

Mum and Dad dragged their heels for three years before admitting that the time had come to say goodbye to shop number three and put an end to the twenty-two years they had worked as shopkeepers. They were tired and beaten. They no longer had the energy to spend another minute looking around a barren space that had once housed a thriving business. Dad, who was now fully retired from Mars, would spend hours just looking out of the front window. Occasionally he would catch the eye of a customer who would throw him a quick smile as they rushed past laden with bags from a Sainsbury's shop. On a visit from university in 1997 my heart sank as I rearranged a few items on the shelves and chatted about the business to my parents, who by this stage looked a little dead behind the eyes.

By 1998 a Co-op had joined the three other supermarkets in Caversham and all were within a few miles of our shop's front door. Despite our copious supply of fresh

* 'Asian corner shops "on the decline"', Dr David McEvoy, Professor of Urban Geography, University of Liverpool, *BBC News 5* (January 2002)

vegetables, meat, dairy, alcoholic and soft drinks, cigarettes and sweets, we were losing the battle to attract the
weekly shopper. Even if we had kept hold of shop number
two, aka the gold mine, we'd have been foolish to think
newspapers and cigarettes could bail us out in our hour of
need.

The customers of yesteryear who had dreamed of
having a car were now replaced by a generation who
rejoiced in owning not just one but often two cars per
household. The freedom of multiple car ownership
enabled one parent to drive to work while the other could
make at least a couple of weekly trips to the town centre
for a day's shopping.

The corner shop owners who had introduced the 'open
all hours' culture to Britain were now buckling under
pressure and struggling to stay open at all. The supermarkets were like special agents who for the past fifty years
had secretly been hiding spies inside corner shops across
the country, taking notes and reporting back to base on
ways to corner the local market. They took our tricks of
the trade, improved and refashioned them, then boldly
passed them off as their own. We may have started trading illegally on a Sunday but it was the supermarkets and
Maggie that made the holy day of rest a thing of the past.
I doubt Maggie's father Mr Roberts, a Methodist preacher,
could have imagined such a thing happening.

We were the ones that had served the community for
generations. But the supermarkets decided to build their
own communities with the offer of club cards and coffee

mornings – all assisted, of course, by little helpers wearing sashes as if they were auditioning for a dodgy beauty pageant in Skegness. We were the ones responsible for allowing children to earn some extra pocket money, employing thousands of boys and girls to do newspaper deliveries across the country. But the supermarkets went one better and just asked carol singing schoolkids to stand in the cold for hours, for free, to entertain the Christmas shoppers with their heartfelt renditions of 'Silent Night'.

But surely they couldn't claim credit for how Britain had become a multicultural, multi-ethnic society thanks to the hundreds of thousands of immigrants who now called Britain their home . . .? Incredibly, they were going to attempt to go one better.

In our shop the average customer would stick to what we termed the 'obvious items' of eggs, bread, flour and milk. These were always on the shopping list as most families' staple items of consumption. The evening meals, however, would vary between fresh and packet food, tinned and frozen options. All, of course, were catered for by our corner shop. The popular items were noticeable by their regularly depleted stock levels. We would frequently run out of supplies of Heinz Baked Beans and Campbell's Soup, the latter being a particular favourite with our senior customers.

Frozen food was pricier than the tinned merchandise but this never seemed to put our customers off, as they'd regularly plough through the big chest freezer deciding on what they wanted to get their gnashers into for supper.

The sight of an overly careless browser getting stuck in was like dragging your fingernails down a chalkboard. Why did people do it? It was excruciating. Just as a prefect watches over the reckless juniors at school, I could never figure out why the perfectly aligned sections could not be kept just so.

Each area of frozen food was distinct. From left to right, it started with the ice creams and lollies, which were easily grabbable, limiting the need to stay longer and potentially mess up the other sections. This was followed by the bags of frozen vegetables, then, occupying the largest and most prominent spot in the middle of the freezer, was a varied choice of frozen ready meals. The most modern addition to the family was a roast dinner, complete with potatoes and gravy. It came in a large cardboard box, so the area previously reserved for frozen chips was squeezed to accommodate this luxury item with a price tag of £5.99. At that price, if it caught the customer's eye, we didn't need to worry too much about the McCain crinkle-cut chips it had pushed aside. Finally, at the far right of the freezer, were multi-packs of chicken legs, lamb cutlets, beef burgers and fish. This end of the freezer was opposite the fresh meat counter, perfectly placed to present a dilemma for the customer: frozen or fresh tonight? We hoped they'd go fresh, as the price mark-up was around 15 per cent more than on the frozen stuff.

But by 1998 not even my perfectly laid out frozen foods or the offer of a free jam roly-poly would entice customers back to us for their weekly shop. While we were rearranging the produce, the supermarkets had been busy taking notes from the immigrant shopkeeper, and emerged with their pièce de resistance: foreign foods.

The supermarkets were going to make the British shopper 'worldly'. It was a knockout blow that took us, seated ringside, by total surprise. The very food that had once been sneered at for a smell that could apparently be detected from miles away was about to be repackaged as exotic, and the British consumer didn't even need a passport for it.

It wasn't something we could've predicted. The supermarkets that stared down at us through their big flashy windows, now copied our chapatti and curry recipes and stashed them in their bag of tricks. The smell of curry was no longer the preserve of an Asian household. The British shopper, who had once looked on the Asian shopkeeper with unease for being so different, was now filling his or her trolley with chicken tikka ready meals and naan bread.

The supermarkets had cottoned on to the fact that a rise in takeaway orders and a busy working life meant an opportunity to cash in on the curious minds who were willing to try a Thai green chicken curry. The more exotic the cuisine, the better. Products and dishes from around the world reflected the extent to which the British had become less parochial. They were now ready to adopt an open attitude to non-British influences. Consumers were hungry for a foreign adventure and would devour the fajita cooking kits, while pesto and tamarind sauce were fast becoming the must-have items in the store cupboard.

It was a trend that was sweeping the nation and the big players were happily encouraging it. The food shopper could now enjoy travelling around the world in eight aisles. From shopping basket to the microwave at home, the exotica would take minutes to prepare. The British consumer would happily settle down to enjoy an episode of *Coronation Street* while tucking into India on a plate. Ironically, our shop was rather English in comparison, and we were about as enticing as a congealed bowl of our tinned chicken and sweetcorn soup.

The time had come to say goodbye. Unless, of course, there were any willing family members who wanted a slice of the corner shop pie. Anyone?

Before judgement is cast upon us, I should just say that 'we', the daughters of shopkeepers, were never asked to take on the shopkeeper mantle. To do so would have been an insult to Mum and Dad's years of hard labour. They did not work tirelessly for twenty-two years, pay for three lots of private school education and university fees for even one of their daughters to utter the words, 'When I grow up, I want to be a shopkeeper.'

We. Did. Not. Want. To. Be. Shopkeepers.

We had watched, heard and endured what corner shop life was all about. To have first-hand experience of shop life is perhaps the most effective way to dissuade the future generation of British Asians from pursuing the same occupation as their parents. There was no chance you'd catch me or my sisters anywhere near one. We had done our shifts in the shop. We had mopped the floors when they needed it. We had picked our parents up when they were stressed. We had filled shelves and religiously conducted the stock take. We had seen and heard what prejudice and racism could look like. And we had had enough pats on the head throughout our childhood to last us a lifetime. With one sister studying French in Metz, the other in law school and me a journalism undergraduate student, the shop's future did not lie in our hands.

There is truth in the stereotypes you may have heard about Asian parents nudging their children towards medicine, dentistry or accountancy. I have yet to meet an Asian shopkeeper who desperately wants their child to follow in their footsteps. Mum and Dad were no exception and they made it very clear from the outset that they'd be immensely proud if there was a doctor, lawyer or accountant in the family. We were not, however, gifted in the fields of science or maths and we ended up following career paths that my parents would never have thought of.

Our education was largely funded by the purchase of newspapers, cigarettes and alcohol. In particular I'd like to pay tribute to Mrs Humphrey for her dedicated consumption of Bell's Whisky that lined my parents' pockets on a daily basis. In fact, we definitely owe the great paying customer a debt of gratitude for investing in us without even realising it. They are in part responsible for our vocations as a landscape gardener, a career in criminal justice and a BBC news presenter.

For my parents, though, saying goodbye to a career that had spanned more than two decades was a hard pill to swallow. They had, like many of their contemporaries, proved all the doubters wrong and successfully run three rather lucrative businesses on their own terms. But this didn't dull the pain of leaving a community that had become like family. To this day, the children of our regular customers, now in their thirties and forties, stop to chat to Mum if they see her passing by. It's amazing how many of them remember our names, even though it's just their faces that I recall.

The corner shop takes more than one family to run it. It requires community support and the kindness of neighbours who offer to do the school pick-ups and drop-offs when help is needed. It operates on the small gestures that make a difference to a gruelling day. It is the thoughtfulness of a customer popping by the shop to wish Mrs Sharma's little girl a happy birthday. My parents served a community for twenty-two years and sixty-five days. The faces of their regular customers are permanently etched in their minds. They are lovely memories but they're mixed with a dose of sadness at how the corner shop business became so weakened in the face of stiff competition.

Shop number three exchanged hands twice before it gave in to a cost-effective business model that has popped up across the country – a branded local convenience store. A Costcutter sign now sits above our old shop where once it read 'V.P. Superstore', symbolising the family business. The local convenience-store franchise, often branded under names like Nisa or Spar, has given the corner shop a lifeline and, crucially, managed to keep it on the street corners of the community. The faces that serve us are the same, but the shop floor and its products are modern and on trend.

The owner of our old shop is Balwant Singh – a shop magnate with years of corner shop graft under his belt. He leans over the shop counter wearing his cool Adidas trainers, blue jeans and Ralph Lauren shirt to boast about his shop empire. It's hard to keep up with his fast, thick London accent, muffled by a long dark beard that seamlessly joins the edges of his tightly bound turban. The cost of being part of a franchise group, he tells me, is easily recouped in sales and there is always safety in numbers against the big supermarkets. Our old shop is one of four that he currently owns in the Greater London area. All operate simultaneously with an army of helpers. Balwant has the ambition to use his grandfather's plot of land in the Punjab to build a huge house for his retirement, which, I'm reliably informed, will be at the age of forty-five, just a few years away. His steely determination convinces me that he is on track to fulfil the dream.

Independent shops have struggled to retain their place on Britain's streets in the face of bulk buying by supermarkets, who needlessly waste food through 'buy one get one free' offers, with the customer falling for the sales trick. So the decision to become part of a wider franchise network is a smart one. The high street has now become a battlefield between the supermarkets and the branded convenience stores. The independent shop owner is being squeezed somewhere in the middle.

As Balwant the Franchise king predicated, the supermarkets that earlier abandoned the town centre have returned to the corner shop's traditional turf on busy residential streets. The spies who have been watching the corner shop since its inception realise that shoppers are now turning their backs on a weekly shopping trip and are once more in favour of frequent top-up shops. We have this change in our shopping habits to thank for the supermarkets' 'local', 'little' and 'express' rebranding of their smaller stores; an attempt to conquer the corner shop terrain that has been working for them so far. However, thanks to immigrants, the corner shop has become the master of reinvention, and this time, it's the turn of the Polish . . .

14

Welcome Mr Nowak

He met Michael Jackson in the corridors of a sprawling stately home. They exchanged a polite hello before the pop star entered a room intoxicated with excited fans, leaving behind a memory burned into the mind of a young Polish man. It was twelve months before the pop icon's untimely death.

This was one of many chance encounters for Bartosz Rybka, who arrived in the UK from Poland in 2007 to work as a receptionist in the luxury stately home of Cliveden in Berkshire. The Italianate mansion sits on the banks of the River Thames covering 374 acres of stunning gardens and parkland, and is often the choice hangout for celebrities. Bart, as he became known in England, regularly exchanged pleasantries with the stars. He proudly recounts how he met Elton John and Sting, as well as observing the wedding of one of the country's finest footballers. Steven Gerrard tied the knot with Alex Curran on 16 June 2007 and Bart worked the entire night shift, serving the select few who were lucky enough to get an invite to the celebrity wedding of the year. But his world today is less chandeliers and candelabras, and more flaki and bigos. The tales of his celebrity encounters amuse the passing trade who enter his corner shop in Reading.

Bartosz is one of more than a million Polish people who are currently living and working in the UK. His arrival in the country and his journey to the corner shop was uncannily similar to the way Dad arrived and made England his home in 1965. One of three, Bart is the middle child of parents who both worked and lived in the Polish town of Rzeszów. The town is 100 miles south west of Krakow and is within easy reach of one of Europe's least explored area of natural beauty – the Bieszczady Mountains. With its sixteenth-century castle and rich history it has become an unlikely tourist destination for many Brits after budget airlines operating in the UK opened a route to the town in 2007. The timing made complete business sense: it coincided with the influx of immigrants from across Eastern Europe and, like Bart, hundreds of thousands of Poles have lined the pockets of Easyjet and Ryanair with countless visits home.

In 2004 Poland joined the European Union and consequently acquired the right to live and work freely in the UK. It was estimated that about 13,000 Poles would arrive in the country in a year, but when immigration was at its peak, almost 100,000 Polish people entered the UK in one twelve-month period.* This new

---

* 'Polish-born people resident in the UK 2001-2010', Office for National Statistics, 25 August 2011

wave of immigrants into the country stirred up conversations of yesteryear. Britain was once again shining a spotlight on its contentious relationship with immigration.

Bart is, he points out, one of thousands of migrants that have come to Britain from Eastern Europe out of choice and not necessity. He does not come from abject poverty, nor has he been pushed out of his homeland by a brutal dictator. Just like my father forty years earlier, Bart came to Britain seeking adventure and the promise of a better wage, armed with the notion that after a few years in Blighty he'd head back home. But something got in the way of his and thousands of other Polish people's plans.

The Asian shopkeeper had helped rescue the unsung hero that is the corner shop from being confined to the history books. Taking it on and shaking it out, they redefined the corner shop with their unique selling point of being open all hours. As Bart maintains decades later, every corner shop owner survives on a USP, and now a new influx of migrants to Britain was eyeing up the corner shop for their own bold ambitions.

It was all well and good adding a slice of lime to Sting's gin and tonic, but working shifts in the hospitality trade was beginning to wear thin. Thanks to a eureka moment on the streets of Slough, another shopkeeper was born. Bart decided to take on a starring role of his own, along with thousands of other migrant workers from Eastern Europe.

A pattern of immigration exists on the outer edges of Londongrad. The spider's web begins at Heathrow Airport, weaving diagonally to Slough, where newly arrived migrants join friends and family in temporary accommodation before spinning a promise of a better opportunity, often in Reading. Bart describes Slough as 'particularly dodgy' and we laugh at the urgency with which both he and my parents were keen to leave the town. Though Reading is no less dodgy in parts, Bart says its appeal lies in its ability to be far enough away from the airport to forget the world you've left behind, yet still close enough to get there easily if things go pear-shaped.

Bart never had to wait for a reminder of home until one drab afternoon in Slough in 2010. There are many Polish delicacies and one enjoyed the world over is a good Polish sausage, which Bart and his compatriots were always able to buy from a particular shop in Slough that enjoyed a healthy clientele of Polish customers, eager to get their hands on the hundreds of products that reminded them of home. One day the queue to enter the shop stretched some 500 yards down the street and attracted much attention from onlookers who were keen to see what all the fuss was about. For Bart, to have to queue like this just to get your hands on some simple Polish sausage was an abomination. But the hour he spent waiting afforded him much thinking time, and it was at this point that he realised he had stumbled upon a USP that would bring him and his friends into a world that had previously been dominated by brown faces. What had begun as an ordinary day for picking up sausages became a moment that planted a seed of ambition in Bart's mind, and would set the course of his life for the next ten years.

Bart was keen to transfer the long man-hours of the hospitality trade into a venture that he could call his own, where he called the shots and could capitalise on a potential business opportunity. The corner shop folded its arms and gave a smug grin. 'Here we go again,' it thought, as it watched yet another immigrant community grapple with an arduous work regime and the promise of plenty . . .

Not one to put all his eggs in one basket, Bart carried on working nights at Cliveden House until the first corner shop he acquired with his friends in Maidenhead could prove it was worthy of a full-time shopkeeper. Bart fondly refers to Maidenhead as a ghost town. It was a place where nothing happened, but as a testing ground for corner shop life, it did the job. The boys wrestled with the daily stock take, fussy customers and a new work routine that made the hospitality trade resemble a leisurely stroll down a quaint country lane. But after a while Bart was armed with the skills necessary to take on a corner shop in a more challenging environment, or so he thought.

With a population of 200,000 people, Reading is home to a burgeoning Polish community. 4,000 Poles call the town home and they are predominantly found in the West

Reading area.* Like the Asian immigrants before them, the new generation of shopkeepers have established their businesses on the notorious Oxford Road. Since the 1960s the Oxford Road has served Britain's new immigrants. It's one of the most densely populated and diverse streets in the whole of the UK. It has always been the perfect example of what the immigration cycle looks like at any given point in the history of Britain. You can buy anything along the Oxford Road, and if you can't buy it here it probably doesn't exist, or so the locals would tell you. Any type of illegal drug and ladies of the night are also readily available, despite numerous attempts by the authorities to clean up the street.

Here no one can lay claim to dominating the corner shop market. More than seventy shops line a street that stretches 1.2 miles west of Reading town centre. Indians, Pakistanis, Somalis, Afro-Caribbeans, Ghanaians and Poles all live side by side, jostling for business. It's a scene that is replicated on many urban streets of Britain today.

Immigrant communities have always taken on small retail spaces, working long hours to earn a living as independent traders. It's not just corner shops that have become a staple of British life. For example, in the noughties there was an explosion of Vietnamese nail bars across the country. In much the same way as the corner

* '2011 Census: Key Statistics for local authorities in England and Wales', Office for National Statistics, 2012

shop business model, the nail bars are open long hours, seven days a week and are predominantly run by immigrants. With a 'no appointment required' service and attractive prices, business is thriving and the Vietnamese community are laying claim to be the next big success story.

But much as it did for Indian and Ugandan Asian immigrants in the 1960s and 1970s, it's the corner shop that remains a lifeline for many immigrant communities who continue to carve out their place in Britain. Refugees who have fled civil war in Sri Lanka can now be seen behind shop counters, as can many in the Afghan community, who have left a homeland burdened by war to seek a better life abroad. People from all over the world can be spotted opening the shutters of a local shop in the early hours of the morning – willing to work hard for an honest living.

For Bart it made business sense to set up shop slap bang in the heart of this community that was already home to ten other Polish shops. Bart's shop sits proudly at a corner junction, and a gold font upon a glossy black background announces 'Polskie Delikatesy', sparking overtones of Oscar night in Hollywood. There is little Hollywood glamour on the inside, mind you, but there is drama nonetheless. Each shelf is stacked high with hundreds of Polish branded products all battling for the title of 'most colourful'. The low-level lighting builds to a crescendo as you venture past the indecipherable crisp packets and chocolates to a bright neon light that illuminates a counter abundantly stocked with fresh meats and cheeses.

To my expert eye, it is perfectly laid out. The alcohol and cigarettes are positioned near the counter and a friendly employee stands ready for action with the widest grin and twinkly blue eyes. As I bestow praise upon Bart's empire he is quick to tell me that the store is to be refurbished within three weeks to encompass the entire building next door. To be a shopkeeper requires a shrewd business sense, and Bart has quickly come to terms with what's needed to excel in this domain. Holding on to his first shop in Maidenhead and adding two more in Reading, his decision to go forth and multiply is paying off handsomely.

But some things about corner shop life never change. Bart dedicates seventy to eighty hours a week to the shop, and it's a stark reminder that while the face behind the counter may change, the inner workings of this great British institution do not. Some burdens of corner shop life have been eased with the advent of the digital age, though. Huge warehouses specialising in Polish products offer an online service that deliver goods direct to a shopkeeper's doorstep, a lifeline for Bart when trying to juggle his empire. There are more than a thousand products in each of his stores. He is, I tell him, missing out on the cash and carry runs that can be the source of much family enjoyment. He ignores my comment, however, perhaps assuming some considerable stupidity on my part for insinuating that any joy could be gleaned from such a time-consuming activity.

It seems English customers do not shy away from Bart's great Polish empire, and he boasts an impressive 30 to 40 per cent non-Eastern European customer base. They particularly enjoy the fresh bread and cheap prices, he informs me. With a promise to branch out into English-labelled products once the shop has been refurbished, Bart is already eyeing up another business opportunity.

Walking out of his shop I felt a smidgen of jealousy as I thought back to the moment Mum and Dad pulled down the shutters for good as tumbleweed rolled past their shop door. If only we had done things a little differently. Perhaps the previous proprietors of the corner shops we'd owned had felt the same sentiment . . . regret.

The corner shop, however, has little time for contrition. It knows only too well that the secret to its success lies in fresh hands and a new way of thinking. For the Asian shopkeeper, our unique selling point, aside from selling Christmas decorations throughout the year, was the 'open all hours' culture and a vigorous work ethic that was lauded by politicians as an example of the great British entrepreneur. But with that modus operandi no longer exclusive to the corner shop market, today's generation of shopkeepers have had to think of something else to stay ahead of the competition. Polish, Latvian and Romanian shops have taken more risks with the business model than my parents did and ventured daringly into uncharted waters.

We gave the public what we essentially thought they wanted. Slices of hand-cut gammon steak with tinned pineapple, or cans of Whiskas and Pedigree Chum. We didn't shake things up by introducing a whole new line of products for fear of pushing an existing customer base away. Our friends from Eastern Europe have not followed the same path. They make no apology for serving specialist items destined to remain within the hands of their communities. It is a bold move to separate from the mainstream consumer and to cater for the homesick immigrant living off a specialist supply of flaki, bigos and pierogi. But the gamble has paid off. The USP has satisfied a demand to cater for the needs of hundreds of thousands of Poles, Latvians, Bulgarians and Romanians who now call Britain home.

Once a specialist niche, now the Polish stores are attracting the curiosity of the British shopper who is brave enough to cross the threshold to appreciate how cheap some of their products are and how actually they might be a serious contender for a weekly shop. Unsurprisingly, the supermarket has eagerly followed the rise of the Polish supermarket and the changing face of Britain's local stores. Many of the big supermarkets are stocking Polish brands, and Heinz introduced its own Pudliszki range of tinned food, while beers such as Tyskie and Lech are selling in greater quantities than ever before.

Given the history, the supermarkets entering a niche market ought to send shivers down the spine of a local shopkeeper, but if anything this time around the supermarkets might actually be directing custom towards small businesses. By taking an interest in stocking specialist foods, the supermarkets are doing the independent trader a favour, since a much wider customer base is learning about what might be happening down the road by perusing the aisles of interesting-looking produce from the safety of a neon-lit powerhouse.

It's bittersweet for the old guard of the corner shop. Asian shopkeepers were very much under the impression that they had to sell milk, bread and eggs to keep the customer happy and were completely unprepared when the supermarkets barrelled in selling 'foreign' foods in the 1980s and 1990s. It closed them down, but is now paving the way for today's new shopkeepers to make the most of a customer who has become more acclimatised to food beyond the British staples.

A supermarket can sell a thousand chicken tikka masalas or cases of Polish beer, but it will never be able to replicate the shopkeeper–customer bond that has been the cornerstone of corner shop life. A Polish shopkeeper can tell you all about the food they sell, how to cook it and give you a lesson in Polish culture in the five minutes it takes you to walk around one aisle of a giant supermarket. It's much the same experience if you walk the streets of Southall and marvel at the bargain prices for costume jewellery and glittery shoes. While the supermarkets are busy undercutting the prices of the local stores, the shopkeepers in Bradford or Leicester have traded a pound of apples and pears at cheap prices for decades. It remains one of the best-kept secrets in the land. But perhaps the idea of a specialist corner shop adds suspicion in the

245

minds of those who haven't subscribed to it about what's going on inside these stores. Don't be afraid: what you'll find in these places are friendly faces with fresh produce at jaw-droppingly low prices.

The latest corner shop takeover by this new generation of Eastern European immigrants once again propelled the issue of immigration towards national debate. Politicians and the media declaring that rising unemployment in 2010 was a result of the influx of immigration made these new corner shop proprietors highly visible, unable to hide from public scrutiny. Just like in the 1960s, 1970s and 1980s, a scapegoat was needed to explain a country with rising unemployment and an overused and under-resourced national health service. Britain's immigration situation was about to make headline news. Again.

In the lead-up to 23 June 2016 the issue of immigration became one of the most debated and divisive aspects of the Brexit question, as Britain asked its citizens to decide whether or not they wanted to remain part of the European Union. The rhetoric that surfaced from the Leave campaign resembled chapters stolen from the history books on the immigration debate that circled my parents like vultures. Concerns about changing neighbourhoods, exemplified by Polish shops such as Bart's standing tall in the community, became a key point in a dark debate. Of course it had little to do with the primary issues of what Britain might look like after exiting the European Union.

The Vote Leave campaign promised a fantasy world where all foreigners played nicely and immigration was dutifully contained. Media campaigns claimed Britain was at breaking point. Adverts were published by the UK Independence Party (UKIP) showing refugees queuing at Europe's borders with a slogan, 'We must break free of the EU and take back control.' The message was clear: if Britons voted Leave during the EU referendum they could stop such people from entering the country. The reality is that Britain's withdrawal from the European Union is a far more complex debate than simply asking who left the gates open when the refugees came in, but that didn't seem to matter. We were back to the blood-sucking days of Idi Amin and the bloodied rivers of Enoch Powell. We were back to the worries of a government playing tag with the immigrant. We were back to the same place that shouted the word 'Paki' on the streets of Britain.

The referendum reopened a dark chapter in Britain's relationship with the immigrant, appearing to offer a chance to settle old scores. It was a case of déjà vu for the shopkeeper. The mantra of the right-wing fascists in the 1980s of 'White jobs for white people' was now replaced with 'British jobs for British people'. When the national mood turns sour, the shopkeeper is always the first to know, but Bart understood the survival technique of the shopkeepers who had gone before him: keep your mouth shut, your ears and eyes open and never offer an opinion.

Britain voted by 51.89 per cent to 48.11 per cent in favour of leaving the European Union, and just a few days later, racist graffiti appeared on the front door of the Polish Cultural Association in Hammersmith. And this was far from being an isolated incident: in the four weeks after the referendum result was declared, more than 6,000 racist hate crimes were reported to the National Police Chiefs' Council,* with little distinction between black, brown or white immigrants – in the perpetrators' eyes, we were all outsiders.

Another unsavoury reminder about the uneasy relationship between the UK and its immigrants came in 2018, when a new scandal hit the headlines involving the so-called Windrush generation. In 1948, 492 workers from Jamaica, Trinidad and Tobago and other islands arrived at Tilbury Docks in the UK on board the MV *Empire Windrush* as a response to post-war labour shortages in the UK. All were British citizens guaranteed rights under the Immigration Act of 1971. In the following decades the Windrush generation put down roots, setting up homes and families and adopting Britain as their home. But the paperwork of those granted a leave to remain was not kept by the Home Office and the Windrush generation found themselves on the wrong side of the law. The storm blew up in 2018 when Prime Minister Theresa May attempted to adopt a hostile environment policy on immigration, and the resulting efforts to stamp out illegal immigrants and reach lower targets lifted the lid off the

* National Police Chiefs Council data published by BBC News Online, 22 July 2016

Windrush scandal. Without detailed records of their arrival, they have been treated as undocumented migrants, denied access to healthcare, jobs, and education and in some cases threatened with deportation. People who had served the nation for decades were being told they had never belonged here. The number of Windrush cases reported to the Home Office has exceeded 5,000[*] and they are yet to be resolved.

This atmosphere is also worrying for millions of EU citizens like Bart, who fear they may face similar treatment after Brexit. When Poland joined the EU family in 2004, the influx of immigrants to the UK left an indelible mark on British culture. It is the way of immigration. Polish has replaced Welsh as the UK's second most common language. And Poland remains the most common non-UK country of birth, taking over from India in 2015 and reflecting a longer-term migration trend.[†]

An unbridled work ethic and determination to succeed means that this young generation of shopkeepers have earned their right to be part of the corner shop story. Bart's home town in Poland is undergoing a tourist boom and he has no doubt that, armed with ten years of entrepreneurial skills, he will find work when he eventually returns there. But he does not want to be turfed off his shop empire by a decision that is forced upon him.

[*] Home Office data, *Guardian*, 25 May 2018
[†] 'Population of the UK by country of birth and nationality: 2017', Office for National Statistics

Ever the optimist, Bart believes that within five years we will be fussing over nothing and he will have expanded his three shops to thirty across the country. He also predicts that Brussels and Westminster will still be doing battle over the terms of Britain's exit from the EU and we will all have fallen into a self-induced coma out of sheer exasperation.

15

The Nine Lives of a Corner Shop

'*A cat has nine lives. For three he plays, for three he strays, and for the last three he stays.*'

Old English proverb

If the corner shop has nine lives, by my estimation we are currently on life number six. So far it has battled its way through a challenging landscape littered with giant obstacles, perverse legislation and political upheaval. As we've explored, the corner shop is intertwined with the immigration cycle in Britain, and to lose one would be to cut off the blood supply to the other. The Polish supermarkets and Vietnamese nail bars on Britain's streets are shining examples of how to navigate today's market.

Thousands of families pour their hearts and souls into spaces that, on the face of it, seem ordinary but actually contain a myriad of essential items that we need on a daily basis. We can only stand back and admire the way in which they have yet again breathed life into the community. For sixty years the corner shop has continued its close affiliation with immigration in Britain and celebrates a bond that has endured the passing of time and competition. Brexit looms and brings with it a heavy burden of anxiety for the shopkeeper. But this, and an eighty-hour working week with early-morning wake-up calls and late-night trading, has not put off a new generation of shopkeepers. They are much needed additions to the corner shop family.

The faces behind the counter may have changed in the past eighty years, but the essence of shop life remains the same. Really, it begins with you.

At the age of seven you exit the shop devouring an ice cream dribbling onto the newspaper you were sent to collect for your mum. By fifteen you're experimenting with rollies or cigarettes. Turned away by the supermarket for being underage, you desperately try to convince the local shopkeeper that you and your mates are old enough. At twenty-three, en route to a party, you head to the only place you know will be open, desperately seeking the bag of Doritos and jar of salsa that you should've picked up earlier. The dips were your only contribution! By thirty you are attempting to bake a cake but have forgotten the unwaxed lemons and tub of mascarpone. You arrive at the corner shop seeking salvation. At forty-two you're in hot pursuit of sourdough but instead settle for wholemeal bread and a cheeky pack of smokes. In your fiftieth year you grudgingly part with your cash knowing you forgot three items from your online shop and won't benefit from the special offers this month. And at sixty-five you walk in for that pint of milk and a good natter about the weather. The corner shop manufactures relationships and memories. Other businesses have tried but failed to capture hearts and imaginations in the same way.

The supermarket, which arrived in the 1950s as subtly as Donald Trump on the porch of the White House, has been the biggest threat to its existence, and for decades Goliath has trodden on the corner shop without apology or acknowledgement. The promise of an online delivery to your door has also proved popular – a blow to the corner shop and the supermarkets alike. With the lure of convenience we are less interested in a big weekly trip to a shop. The dotcom revolution of the noughties has forever changed our shopping habits: internet sales now make up 18.2 per cent of all retail sales in Britain* and the effect on the high street has been clear. Much-loved stores have folded and the supermarket that downsized in an effort to muscle in on the high street has been caught in the middle.

But according to the Waitrose Food and Drink Report 2017, one in ten people decide what to buy for an evening meal just before they eat it – often stopping to shop for it on the way home from work. The corner shop is perfectly poised to serve this passing trade. And if the internet beast has become the latest obstacle to overcome, it is still some way off replicating the level of trust customers feel when

* Office for National Statistics data, published in the *Daily Telegraph*, 16 February 2018

they walk into a local shop. In a bizarre twist of fate, customers are increasingly turning their backs on the conglomerates.

We no longer weigh bags of sugar or dole out spoon-fuls of fig juice to get the bowels moving. Turmeric is now the UK's top-selling spice (overtaking cinnamon) and grapes have overtaken apples to become Britain's bestsell-ing fruit.[*] But the threat to supermarket sales is not a result of our sophisticated taste buds; the supermarkets' egos are to blame. Preoccupied with each other and perpetually engaged in price wars and a 'multiply and conquer' strategy, they have disregarded the internet, the local shop and the German discounters at their peril.

Supporting the local is also on trend and the ethical shopper is emerging ever more strongly, advocating plastic-free, gluten-free and environmentally sourced produce. The corner shop may not be a farm shop, with over-inflated prices and the promise of everything organic. But supporting the underdog is very British, everyone loves a trier and it's become popular to support the independent shop, which is now considered a worthy recipient of your cash. Perhaps after all these years and in the face of an uncertain future, Britain is ready to celebrate its unsung hero. The bricks-and-mortar pres-ence of a neighbourhood shop with affordable prices is still a business model to be reckoned with. The corner shop market is expected to increase by 17 per cent to

[*] 2017 Report, *The Grocer,* 18 December 2017

£44 billion over the next five years.* The 'pop to the shop' routine is back in vogue.

The climate that welcomed a friendly shopkeeper as the bastion of community life has undoubtedly changed, but you still keep coming.

On a Sunday morning, you arrive in your pyjamas to grab the newspaper and its supplements, which have been inserted by a dutiful shopkeeper by hand. You take advantage of the special offer to repair the cracked screen on your phone at a ridiculously low price and grin from ear to ear when the shopkeeper tells you it will be ready in an hour. You walk in when you find yourself on the wrong side of town, desperate to get change for the parking meter. The shopkeeper, listening to indecipherable music on a barely functioning radio, happily obliges your request for change from a twenty pound note, provided you've bought a pack of chewing gum as a gesture of goodwill. With a 100 per cent mark-up on the recommended retail price, the gum purchase draws a wry smile from the shopkeeper.

Against the odds the corner shop continues to serve a community from a tiny little space at the junction of two streets. It's where the art of conversation flourishes and global politics, lottery numbers and headlines from the morning newspapers are still enthusiastically debated.

If you are in Reading, at least once or twice a week you can spot an elderly Indian couple squeezing the courgettes

* 'Local Shop Report 2016', The Association of Convenience Stores

in Aldi and sizing up the tomatoes in Tesco. They still scour the supermarket shelves searching for 'best buys' and lamenting the extortionate prices on offer. Old habits die hard. They don't miss the early morning wake-up calls or the painfully long hours. What Mum and Dad miss most about the shops is you, their customers.

Look a little closer and hidden behind the shop counter you might see a young girl with bunches peering up at you, wondering why you have entered her world. Maybe the shop is breeding the next generation of journalists who will discover how shop-floor banter can be a highly useful means of information gathering. Or maybe there is another prime minister-in-waiting getting a front-row seat to the way society and the customer operates.

Whether the corner shop can survive long term depends on the unwritten pact between shopkeeper and customer. If obeyed, it shall continue to serve a nation.

'Special Offer anyone? Buy any sausage roll and a newspaper for ONLY £2.99!'

Dear Shop,

I'm sorry for some of the things I have said about you.

I know I said I hated you but I didn't mean it really. I hope the next people that come here will be nice. They might have to paint our bedroom and fix the gaps in the floorboards.

We are moving to a big house with a garden and I think we might even get a dog! I promise to come and visit you all the time.

I will miss you very much.

Babita (aged 10¾ years)

Acknowledgements

From the outset my publisher Kate Hewson was charmed by the history of the corner shop and insisted that a book be written about it. I'm immensely grateful to Kate and all the team at Two Roads that we ended up on this journey together. My agent, the true gent that is Rory Scarfe, has been a pillar of support from the very beginning. Thank you, Rory, for helping me navigate the wonderful literary world.

Friends, work colleagues and strangers all had a corner shop story to tell and in turn they spurred me on through the countless drafts and edits. I'd particularly like to thank Bill Hayton for his humour when I'd complain that 'no-one told me it would be this difficult!'. A special mention to Katie Amos at Reading Central Library, Stephen Weir at the Ulster Transport and Folk Museum, and Ronan Hegarty from The Grocer. And for providing the measurements of Margaret Thatcher's bedroom in Grantham, thank you Sandra Good.

The biggest thanks goes to my family of whom I asked countless questions. My Mum and Dad who without refusal answered all my questions, time and time again. The hours we spent chatting about their lives and my childhood completed a picture that is now filled with precious memories. To the Anchals for their animated account of life in East Africa, I love you all dearly. And to Adam, my husband and champion, you pushed me on, picked me up and stood by me with unconditional support throughout. I love you.

To every corner shop owner in the country, you inspire me on a daily basis. We belong to a special club and it's an honour to be able to celebrate it in the pages of this book.

About the Author

Babita Sharma is a journalist, TV presenter and news anchor for the BBC. She presents *Newsday* on BBC World News, covering major global news events including the Trump-Kim Summit in Singapore, the EU Referendum, the Rio Olympics and the award-winning BBC *100 Women* series. Passionate about diversity and mental health issues, Babita mentors BAME journalists and also works with charity Mind.

Babita presented BBC Two's *Dangerous Borders: The Story of India & Pakistan*. The documentary series took Babita to the India/Pakistan border 70 years after partition, following in the footsteps of her family who were directly affected. *The Corner Shop* is her first book. It follows her critically acclaimed documentary *Booze, Beans & Bhajis: The Story of the Corner Shop* broadcast on BBC Four, BBC News Channel and BBC World News. Babita is married and lives in London.